THE
CYCLING
CARTOONIST
AN ILLUSTRATED GUIDE TO
LIFE ON TWO WHEELS

THE CYCLING CARTOONIST

AN ILLUSTRATED GUIDE TO LIFE ON TWO WHEELS

DAVE WALKER

BLOOMSBURY

LONDON · OXFORD · NEW YORK · NEW DELHI · SYDNEY

Bloomsbury Sport
An imprint of Bloomsbury Publishing Plc

50 Bedford Square
London
WC1B 3DP
UK

1385 Broadway
New York
NY 10018
USA

www.bloomsbury.com

First published in 2017
© Dave Walker, 2017

British Library Cataloguing-in-Publication Data
A catalogue record for this book is available from the British Library.

Library of Congress Cataloguing-in-Publication data has been applied for.

ISBN: Hardback: 9781472938893
ePub: 9781472938886
ePDF: 9781472938916

6 8 10 9 7 5

Printed and bound in Great Britain by Bell and Bain Ltd, Glasgow

Bloomsbury Publishing Plc makes every effort to ensure that the papers used in the manufacture of our books are
natural, recyclable products made from wood grown in well-managed forests. Our manufacturing processes conform
to the environmental regulations of the country of origin.

To find out more about our authors and books visit www.bloomsbury.com. Here you will find extracts, author interviews,
details of forthcoming events and the option to sign up for our newsletters.

INTRODUCTION TO THE PROJECT

I AM GOING TO EXPLAIN THE WORLD OF CYCLING USING VARIOUS DIAGRAMS. INFORMATION HAS BEEN GATHERED FROM THE FOLLOWING SOURCES:

READING CYCLING MAGAZINES FROM THE 1980S

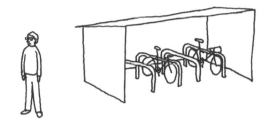

LOITERING IN THE VICINITY OF THE BIKE SHEDS

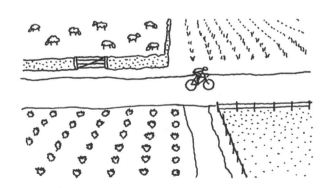

HOURS AND HOURS ON THE OPEN ROAD

HIDING BEHIND THE VILLAGE HALL CURTAINS DURING THE 10 MILE TIME TRIAL SIGN-ON

20 REASONS

TO LOVE CYCLING

① LOVELY PEOPLE

② BEAUTIFUL TECHNOLOGY

③ BRIGHTLY-COLOURED JERSEYS

ADVERTISING THINGS YOU HAVE NEVER HEARD OF

④ THE WAY THE PEDALS CLIP INTO THE SHOES THESE DAYS

⑤ IT KEEPS CAFÉS GOING ON SUNDAY MORNINGS

CAFÉ

⑥ THE EUPHORIA THAT COMES FROM GOING DOWNHILL VERY QUICKLY

⑦ IT IS INCREDIBLY GOOD FOR YOU

(FULL EXTENT OF MY MEDICAL KNOWLEDGE)

⑧ IT IS A QUICK WAY TO GET FROM A TO B

A · · B

⑨ IT IS AN ANTIDOTE TO LOW MORALE

⑩ FASCINATING RACE STRATEGIES

(TOO COMPLEX TO EXPLAIN)

⑪ THE CHALLENGE OF SCALING MOUNTAINS

⑫ YOU CAN GO ANYWHERE*

*OBVIOUSLY NOT ANYWHERE

⑬ THE IMPRESSIVE SIGHT OF A PELOTON SWOOSHING PAST

⑭ SEEING A RACE UP CLOSE

⑮ IT IS FUN TO GET LOST

NO IDEA

⑯ EATING A LOT AND BURNING IT OFF

[FOOD - IN CASE NOT OBVIOUS]

⑰ IT IS NON-POLLUTING

SOME MILD ODOUR BUT THAT'S IT

⑱ THE POST-RIDE PINT

⑲ IT IS INEXPENSIVE (WELL, FAIRLY)

BIKE SHOP

⑳ THE FEELING OF THE WIND IN YOUR HAIR*

*YOU MAY LIKE TO WEAR A HELMET

MODES OF TRANSPORT

OBJECTIVELY COMPARED

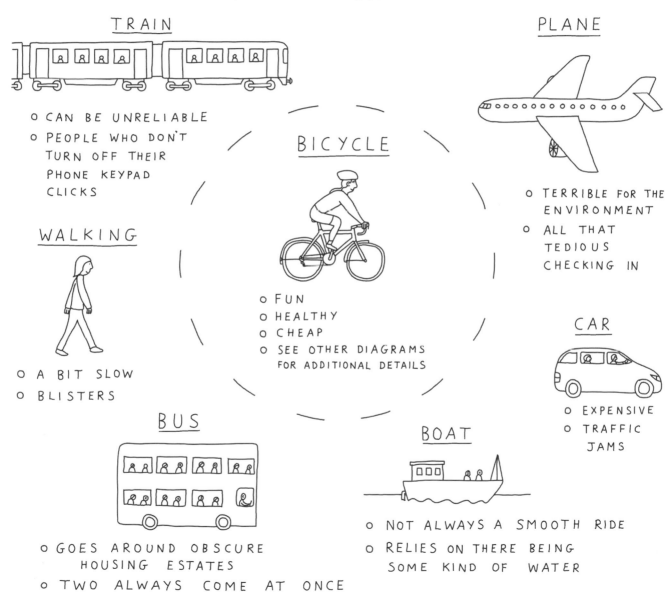

TRAIN

o CAN BE UNRELIABLE
o PEOPLE WHO DON'T TURN OFF THEIR PHONE KEYPAD CLICKS

PLANE

o TERRIBLE FOR THE ENVIRONMENT
o ALL THAT TEDIOUS CHECKING IN

BICYCLE

o FUN
o HEALTHY
o CHEAP
o SEE OTHER DIAGRAMS FOR ADDITIONAL DETAILS

WALKING

o A BIT SLOW
o BLISTERS

CAR

o EXPENSIVE
o TRAFFIC JAMS

BUS

o GOES AROUND OBSCURE HOUSING ESTATES
o TWO ALWAYS COME AT ONCE

BOAT

o NOT ALWAYS A SMOOTH RIDE
o RELIES ON THERE BEING SOME KIND OF WATER

JOURNEYS

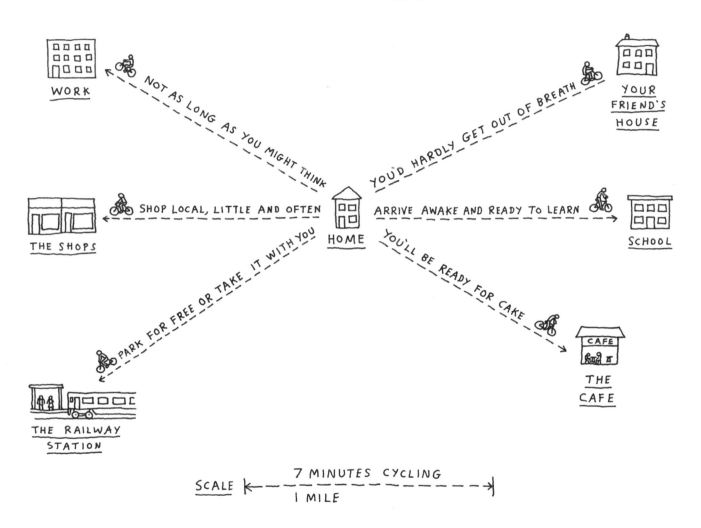

WORK

NOT AS LONG AS YOU MIGHT THINK

YOU'D HARDLY GET OUT OF BREATH

YOUR FRIEND'S HOUSE

SHOP LOCAL, LITTLE AND OFTEN

THE SHOPS

HOME

ARRIVE AWAKE AND READY TO LEARN

SCHOOL

PARK FOR FREE OR TAKE IT WITH YOU

YOU'LL BE READY FOR CAKE

CAFE

THE CAFE

THE RAILWAY STATION

SCALE

7 MINUTES CYCLING
1 MILE

HOW LONG WOULD YOUR JOURNEYS BE?

THE PERIODIC TABLE

OF CYCLISTS

SR SERIOUS ROADIE								DC DAILY COMMUTER
TT TIME TRIALLER	FP FORMER PROFESSIONAL					CC CYCLE COURIER	SH DOING THE SHOPPING	SP SUNDAY POOTLER
CX CYCLO-CROSSER	SE SPORTIVE ENTHUSIAST					FH FIXIE HIPSTER	CB CARGO BIKER	FT FOLDER ON TRAIN
MB MOUNTAIN BIKER	CS • CLUBRUN STALWART	B BMX-ER	U UNICYCLIST	LD LONG-DISTANCE ADVENTURER	OV ✳ OCCASIONAL VENTURER	MA MAGNIFICENTLY BEARDED	SB 'SIT UP AND BEG' RIDER	HB ♎ HIRE BIKE RIDER
DH DOWNHILLER	NM [?] NEW CLUB MEMBER	ST STUNTS AND TRICKS	TC TANDEM COUPLE	PC III PREFERS CARBON	SO SUMMER ONLY	CH ⁘ ≡ CHATTING IN CAFE	FO FAMILY OUTING	KT KIDS IN TRAILER
TR TRACK RACER	RB RETRO BICYCLIST	IH ○ IGNORES HIGHWAY CODE	T TRICYCLIST	SW □ STEEL ALL THE WAY	PH PUSHING UP HILLS	RR ! ROAD RAGER	SS STABILISERS	DB DOG IN BASKET

S • SPRINTER	C CLIMBER	D ~ DOMESTIQUE	DS DIRECTEUR SPORTIF	TM ↓ TEAM MECHANIC	RM RACE MARSHAL	WV ✳ • WILLING VOLUNTEER

KEY

• SOLID	♎ HEAVY METALS	✳ RARE	≡ INACTIVE
~ HOLDS LIQUID	□ METALOID	[?] UNKNOWN PROPERTIES	↓ EXISTS UNDER PRESSURE
⁘ NOBLE GASSES	III NON METALS	! HIGHLY REACTIVE	○ QUITE DENSE

BUYING A NEW BIKE

WAYS TO SOFTEN THE BLOW

DEMONSTRATE THAT THIS BIKE
REALLY ISN'T THAT EXPENSIVE

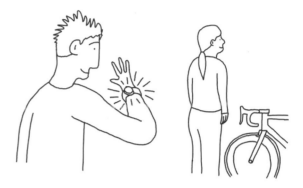

TURN A BLIND EYE TO PARTNER'S
PURCHASES OF [INSERT NAME OF LUXURY ITEM]

MONEY
SAVED IN
THE LONG RUN

A LOT CHEAPER
THAN A
SPORTS CAR

HEALTH

POTENTIAL
OLYMPIC
MEDAL

GETS ME
OUT OF
THE HOUSE

EXPLAIN THE MANY BENEFITS

SEVEN YEARS OF HARD TOIL

BICYCLES

WHY YOU MIGHT NEED MORE THAN ONE

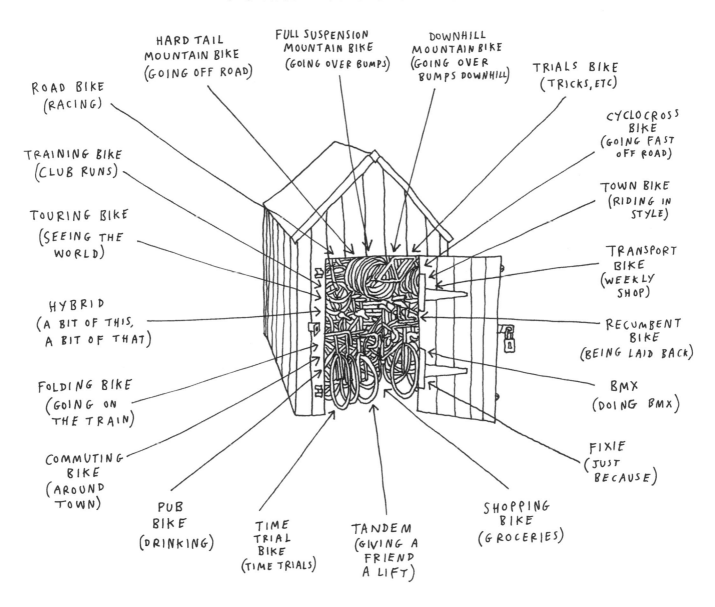

ROAD BIKE (RACING)

HARD TAIL MOUNTAIN BIKE (GOING OFF ROAD)

FULL SUSPENSION MOUNTAIN BIKE (GOING OVER BUMPS)

DOWNHILL MOUNTAIN BIKE (GOING OVER BUMPS DOWNHILL)

TRIALS BIKE (TRICKS, ETC)

CYCLOCROSS BIKE (GOING FAST OFF ROAD)

TRAINING BIKE (CLUB RUNS)

TOURING BIKE (SEEING THE WORLD)

TOWN BIKE (RIDING IN STYLE)

TRANSPORT BIKE (WEEKLY SHOP)

HYBRID (A BIT OF THIS, A BIT OF THAT)

RECUMBENT BIKE (BEING LAID BACK)

FOLDING BIKE (GOING ON THE TRAIN)

BMX (DOING BMX)

COMMUTING BIKE (AROUND TOWN)

FIXIE (JUST BECAUSE)

PUB BIKE (DRINKING)

TIME TRIAL BIKE (TIME TRIALS)

TANDEM (GIVING A FRIEND A LIFT)

SHOPPING BIKE (GROCERIES)

THE BIKE SHOP

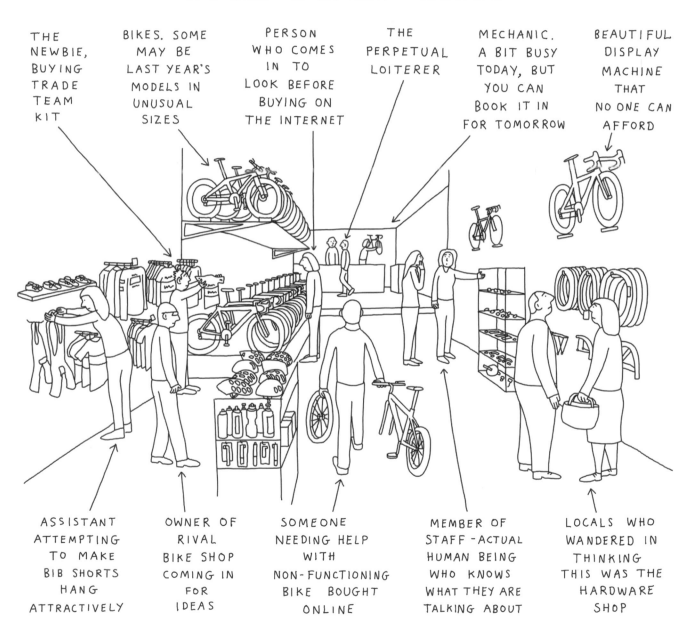

THE NEWBIE, BUYING TRADE TEAM KIT

BIKES. SOME MAY BE LAST YEAR'S MODELS IN UNUSUAL SIZES

PERSON WHO COMES IN TO LOOK BEFORE BUYING ON THE INTERNET

THE PERPETUAL LOITERER

MECHANIC. A BIT BUSY TODAY, BUT YOU CAN BOOK IT IN FOR TOMORROW

BEAUTIFUL DISPLAY MACHINE THAT NO ONE CAN AFFORD

ASSISTANT ATTEMPTING TO MAKE BIB SHORTS HANG ATTRACTIVELY

OWNER OF RIVAL BIKE SHOP COMING IN FOR IDEAS

SOMEONE NEEDING HELP WITH NON-FUNCTIONING BIKE BOUGHT ONLINE

MEMBER OF STAFF - ACTUAL HUMAN BEING WHO KNOWS WHAT THEY ARE TALKING ABOUT

LOCALS WHO WANDERED IN THINKING THIS WAS THE HARDWARE SHOP

MY NEW BICYCLE

WHAT SHOULD IT BE?

SPORTIVE
MEDAL

IT CERTAINLY NEEDS TO BE
A ROAD BIKE SO THAT I CAN
EMULATE MY TOUR DE FRANCE
HEROES (WELL... RIDE SOME SPORTIVES)

I COULD
TAKE A
TENT AND
EVERYTHING

ACTUALLY, IT HAS GOT TO BE
A TOURING BIKE, AS I AM, IF I'M
HONEST, TOO OLD TO RACE, BUT THERE'S
A WHOLE WORLD TO BE EXPLORED

UNDERGROUND
TRAIN PASS
NO LONGER
REQUIRED

THAT SAID, A FOLDING BIKE WOULD
BE BRILLIANT. I COULD TAKE IT
ON THE TRAIN AND OPEN UP ALL
SORTS OF URBAN POSSIBILITIES

INTREPID
EXPLORATION
OF NEARBY
BRIDLE
PATHS

I'VE DECIDED. IT IS DEFINITELY GOING
TO BE A MOUNTAIN BIKE. I DON'T LIKE
RIDING ON THE ROAD MUCH, AND WE LIVE
QUITE NEAR A VERY NICE COUNTRY PARK

REDUCING WEIGHT

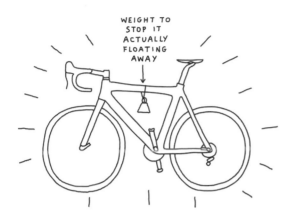

WEIGHT TO
STOP IT
ACTUALLY
FLOATING
AWAY

BUY A LIGHTER BIKE,
COMPONENTS, ETC

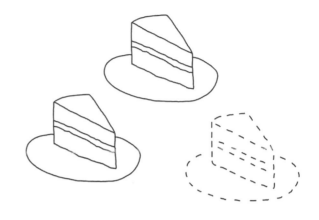

REFUSE THIRD
SLICE OF CAKE

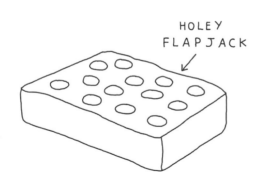

HOLEY
FLAPJACK

DRILL HOLES
IN SNACKS

JETTISON UNNECESSARY ITEMS
AT BEGINNING OF FINAL CLIMB

YOUR NEW WHEELS

PLACES TO HIDE THEM SO YOUR PARTNER DOESN'T FIND OUT

IN THE CAR BOOT

IN THE ROOF

IN PLAIN SIGHT
IN THE HOUSE

PRETEND THEY ARE
A SCULPTURE

KEEP THEM ON
THE BIKE

LEAVE THEM UN-BOUGHT
IN THE SHOP

HOW SERIOUS ARE YOU?

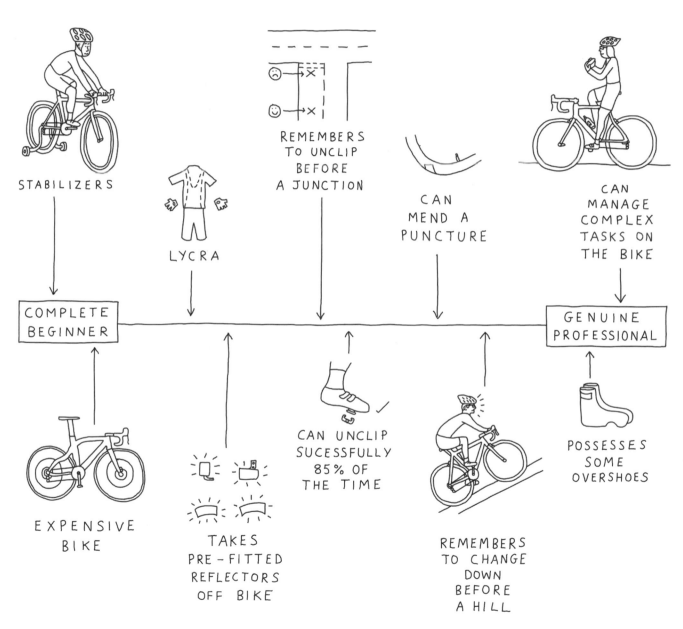

STABILIZERS

LYCRA

REMEMBERS TO UNCLIP BEFORE A JUNCTION

CAN MEND A PUNCTURE

CAN MANAGE COMPLEX TASKS ON THE BIKE

COMPLETE BEGINNER

GENUINE PROFESSIONAL

EXPENSIVE BIKE

TAKES PRE-FITTED REFLECTORS OFF BIKE

CAN UNCLIP SUCESSFULLY 85% OF THE TIME

REMEMBERS TO CHANGE DOWN BEFORE A HILL

POSSESSES SOME OVERSHOES

BECOMING A MAMIL*

*MIDDLE-AGED MAN IN LYCRA

① BE A MAN

(YOU CAN MOST CERTAINLY BE A WOMAN OF COURSE. YOU WILL JUST NEED TO MAKE A MINOR ADJUSTMENT TO THE ACRONYM)

② REACH MIDDLE AGE

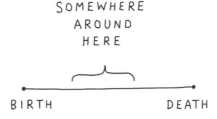

SOMEWHERE AROUND HERE

BIRTH   DEATH

③ ENJOY CYCLING

WOO HOO

④ REALISE THAT CYCLING SHORTS WOULD MAKE THE WHOLE EXPERIENCE FAR MORE COMFORTABLE

WOW. THIS MAKES SUCH A DIFFERENCE

AREA OF PADDING

⑤ LEARN THAT IT IS FAR MORE EFFICIENT TO USE SHOES THAT CLIP INTO THE PEDALS

CLEAT →
PEDAL →

⑥ DECIDE THAT, HAVING GOT THE SHORTS, THE MATCHING JERSEY IS AN ENTIRELY SENSIBLE ADDITION

⑦ MAKE FRIENDS WITH STEVE, WHO HAS NUMEROUS BIKES, ALL MANNER OF KIT, EQUIPMENT, AND SUCHLIKE

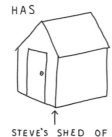

STEVE'S SHED OF BICYCLE DELIGHTS

⑧ RESOLVE TO BE MORE LIKE STEVE

I'M GETTING NEW WHEELS

YES, I THINK I MIGHT GET NEW WHEELS TOO

⑨ YOU ARE MORE OR LESS THERE

OFF-DUTY CYCLISTS

HOW TO SPOT THEM IN THE SUPERMARKET

TURKEY

PASTA

FRESH FRUIT AND VEG

A CERTAIN PERCENTAGE OF FOOD IN GEL FORM

CONTENTS OF TROLLEY

THE WAY THEY PICK UP A BOTTLE

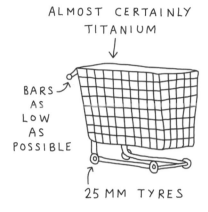

ALMOST CERTAINLY TITANIUM

BARS AS LOW AS POSSIBLE

25 MM TYRES

CHOICE OF TROLLEY

AERO POSITION

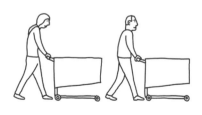

DRAFTING

RIGHT-HAND TROUSER TUCKED INTO SOCK

CYCLING MISTAKES

TO AVOID

EVEN AN ENERGY GEL...

NOT BRINGING
ENOUGH FOOD

DRESSING INAPPROPRIATELY
FOR THE WEATHER

LEAVING SPARE INNER
TUBE AT HOME

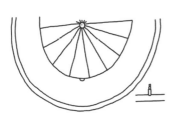

THE WRONG TUBES FOR
DEEP WHEEL RIMS

A LACK OF SUN
PROTECTION

THINKING THAT THAT
POTHOLE WASN'T THAT DEEP

MULTI-STOREY CAR
PARK ERROR

FORGETTING
BIKE

OVERCONFIDENT
JACKET REMOVAL

SADDLE HEIGHT

HOW TO GET IT RIGHT

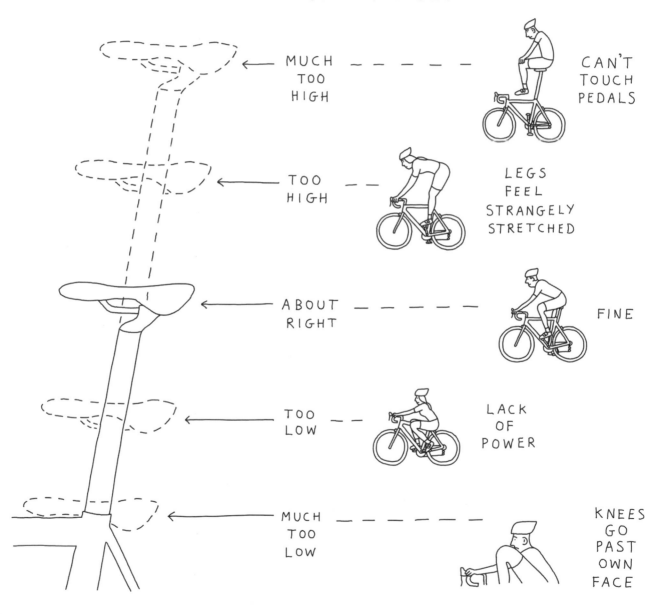

MUCH TOO HIGH — CAN'T TOUCH PEDALS

TOO HIGH — LEGS FEEL STRANGELY STRETCHED

ABOUT RIGHT — FINE

TOO LOW — LACK OF POWER

MUCH TOO LOW — KNEES GO PAST OWN FACE

CYCLE CLOTHING

THE CURRENT STATE OF YOUR KIT

CLEAN

HARDLY WORN

WORN A FEW TIMES

CAN GET AWAY WITH IT

PROBABLY NEEDS A WASH

A BIT TOO FAR GONE

RIDING IN A GROUP

|

TAKE
A
TURN
AT
THE
FRONT

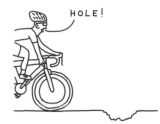

COMMUNICATE
TO
OTHER
RIDERS

RIDE
MORE
THAN
TWO
ABREAST

OVERLAP
WHEELS

PAY
ATTENTION

RIDE
PREDICTABLY

ACCELERATE
WHEN
YOU'RE
ON
THE
FRONT

BRAKE
SUDDENLY

HAND SIGNALS

TURNING RIGHT

SLOWING DOWN

YOUR TURN AT THE FRONT

HOLE

OBSTRUCTION

NEED THE LOO/ TEAM CAR

I'VE WON

GESTURE NOT SHOWN

WHAT THE ?＊$⚡# DO YOU THINK YOU'RE DOING?

23

ON-THE-BIKE ABILITIES

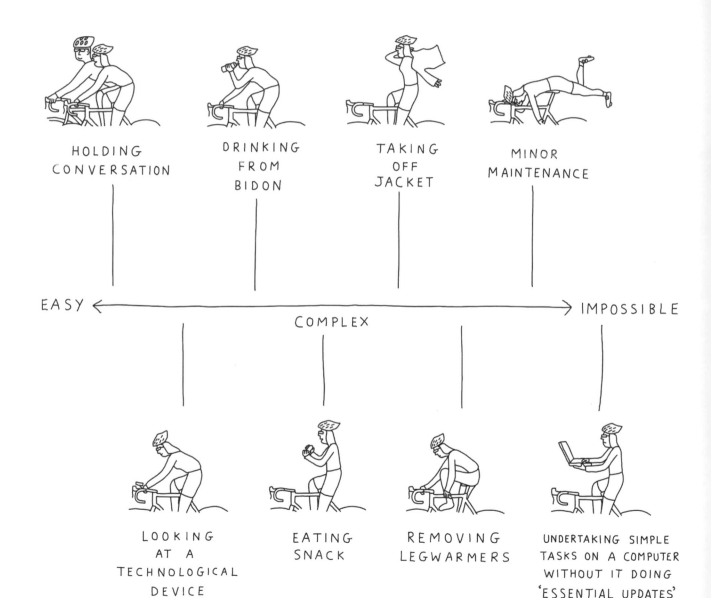

HOLDING CONVERSATION

DRINKING FROM BIDON

TAKING OFF JACKET

MINOR MAINTENANCE

EASY ← COMPLEX → IMPOSSIBLE

LOOKING AT A TECHNOLOGICAL DEVICE

EATING SNACK

REMOVING LEGWARMERS

UNDERTAKING SIMPLE TASKS ON A COMPUTER WITHOUT IT DOING 'ESSENTIAL UPDATES'

ADVANCED SKILLS

BUNNY HOP
(OVER POTHOLE)

NO HANDS
(CAREFUL NOW)

BYSTANDERS.
INCREDIBLY
IMPRESSED

TRACK STAND
(AT THE LIGHTS)

WHEELIE
(SHOWING OFF)

CIRCUS SKILLS
(PASSES TIME ON
THE COMMUTE)

RINGING BELL
(IN A WAY THAT SOUNDS
NON-AGGRESSIVE AND
DOESN'T STARTLE PEDESTRIANS)

CYCLING HABITS

GUARANTEED TO UPSET A PURIST

WEARING WORLD
CHAMPION'S KIT
IF YOU AREN'T ONE

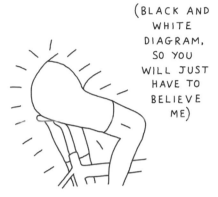

(BLACK AND
WHITE
DIAGRAM,
SO YOU
WILL JUST
HAVE TO
BELIEVE
ME)

SHORTS THAT ARE
A COLOUR
OTHER THAN BLACK

PUTTING
YOUR BIKE
UPSIDE DOWN

WRONGLY-ALIGNED
QUICK
RELEASES

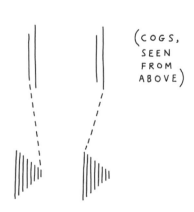

(COGS,
SEEN
FROM
ABOVE)

RIDING WITH
ILL-ADVISED GEAR
COMBINATIONS

RIDING WITH
ILL-ADVISED GEAR
COMBINATIONS

CYCLING VIDEOS

YOU'LL NEVER GUESS WHAT HAPPENED NEXT...

RIDES DOWN
SEEMINGLY
IMPOSSIBLE
CLIFF

SLOWS DOWN
TO PASS
DOG WALKER

BALANCES
ON TOP OF
PARK BENCH

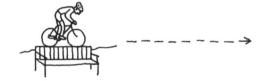 

SITS DOWN
TO ADMIRE
VIEW

JUMPS OVER
IMMENSE
CAVERN

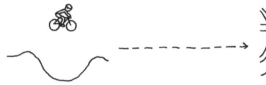 

STOPS TO
ADJUST
SOCKS

SPEEDS DOWN
TECHNICAL
FOREST TRAIL

ARRIVES AT
NEWSAGENT.
GOES IN TO
BUY A PAPER

OFF THE BIKE

WHY I HAVEN'T BEEN OUT RIDING FOR SEVEN AND A HALF WEEKS

	MONDAY	TUESDAY	WEDNESDAY	THURSDAY	FRIDAY	SATURDAY	SUNDAY
WEEK 1	Working	Ill	Terrible excuse	Family commitment	Weather	Family commitment	Family commitment
WEEK 2	Working	Weather	Working	Working	Working	Weather	Terrible excuse
WEEK 3	Working	Ill	Ill	Weather	Terrible excuse	Family commitment	Family commitment
WEEK 4	Working	Working	Weather	Family commitment	Terrible excuse	Bike broken	Bike broken
WEEK 5	Bike broken	Bike broken	Bike broken	Bike broken	Bike broken	Bike broken	Weather
WEEK 6	Weather	Weather	Working	Working	Working	Weather	Family commitment
WEEK 7	Working	Ill	Ill	Ill	Family commitment	Family commitment	Terrible excuse
WEEK 7 AND A HALF	Working	Weather	Working	Terrible excuse			

 WORKING

 BIKE BROKEN

 LOOK AT THE WEATHER

 FAMILY COMMITMENT

 ILL

 MAKING SOME KIND OF TERRIBLE EXCUSE

28

THE LIVING ROOM

REASONS TO STORE YOUR BIKE THERE

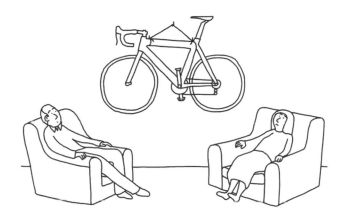

AS A WORK OF ART
ON THE WALL

ADDITIONAL SEATING
FOR VISITORS

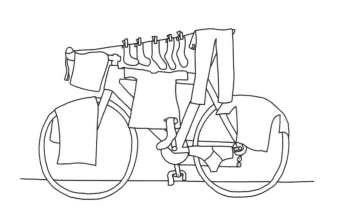

AN EXTRA SPACE
TO HANG LAUNDRY

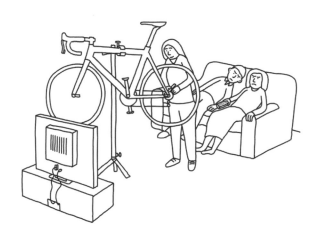

IT IS A NICE WARM PLACE
TO WORK ON IT

CYCLIST GREETINGS

THE NOD

THE NOD AND SMILE

THE RAISED HAND

THE WAVE

THE OVERENTHUSIASTIC
WAVE

THE IGNORE (TOO COOL,
ALSO I AM TRAINING FOR
SOMETHING INCREDIBLY
IMPORTANT AND MUST
NOT BE DISTRACTED)

MINOR CYCLING MISHAPS

STILL NOT GOT THE HANG
OF THESE PEDALS

BIN-BAGS FULL OF SOFT
FURNISHINGS HAVE BEEN
FORTUITOUSLY LEFT
ON THE OUTSIDE
OF THE CORNER

THE CORNER WAS SHARPER
THAN EXPECTED

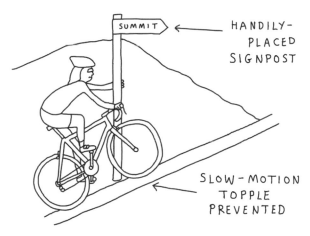

HANDILY-
PLACED
SIGNPOST

SLOW-MOTION
TOPPLE
PREVENTED

ON A HILL. THE GEARS
CRUNCH AND GRIND

FORTUNATELY HADN'T LEFT
THE WELL-CUSHIONED
CONFINES
OF THE
LIVING
ROOM

TRYING TO PUT JACKET
ON WHILST ON THE MOVE

PLANNING YOUR SEASON

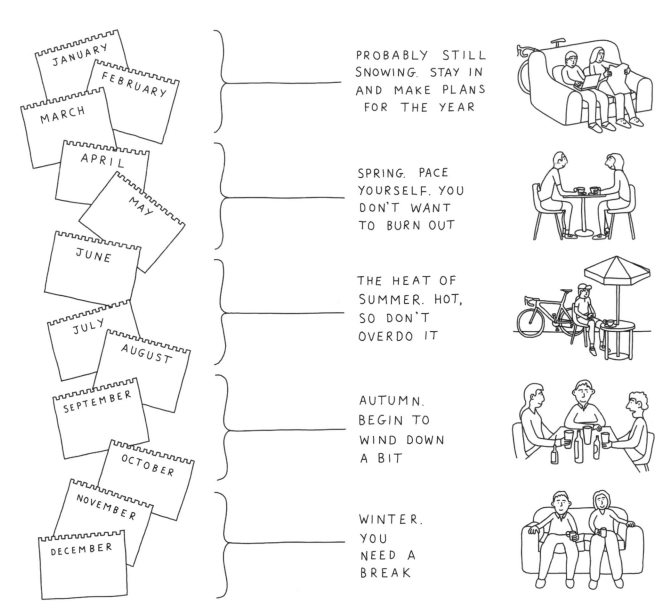

JANUARY
FEBRUARY
MARCH
APRIL
MAY
JUNE
JULY
AUGUST
SEPTEMBER
OCTOBER
NOVEMBER
DECEMBER

PROBABLY STILL
SNOWING. STAY IN
AND MAKE PLANS
FOR THE YEAR

SPRING. PACE
YOURSELF. YOU
DON'T WANT
TO BURN OUT

THE HEAT OF
SUMMER. HOT,
SO DON'T
OVERDO IT

AUTUMN.
BEGIN TO
WIND DOWN
A BIT

WINTER.
YOU
NEED A
BREAK

THE SPORTIVE

THINGS I HAVE SEEN

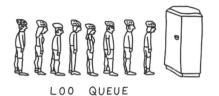

LOO QUEUE

GREEDY FEED-ZONE PARTICIPANT

VERY SERIOUS RIDER, WHO THINKS IT'S A RACE

BIDON IN ROAD

BIDET IN ROAD

CAR!
HOLE!
I USED TO WORK THERE!

SIGNALS FOR THE RIDERS FOLLOWING

$#*@!

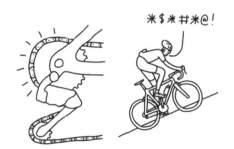

GEARS NOT WORKING ON STEEP CLIMBS (AND ASSOCIATED EXCLAMATIONS)

EXPENSIVE BIKE NOT REALLY HELPING →

RIDER TALKED INTO IT BY A FRIEND. NOW REGRETTING EVERYTHING

ROUTE A
ROUTE B
TAKE ME HOME

SIGNS

MY TROPHY CABINET

THE GAPS EXPLAINED

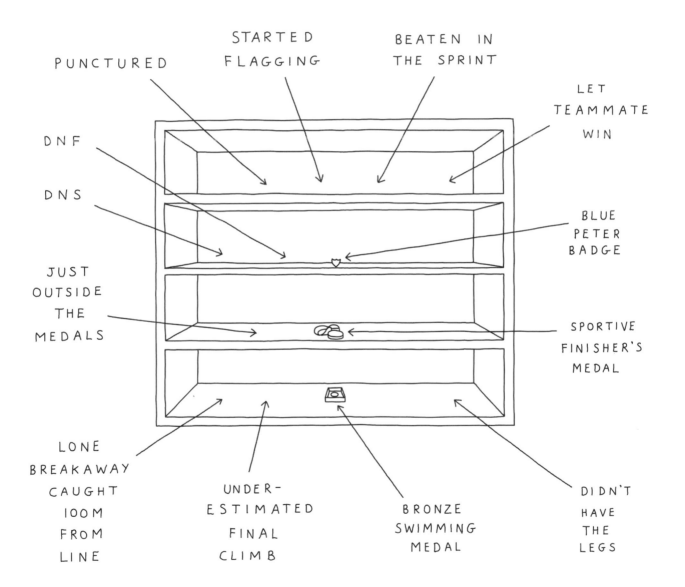

PUNCTURED

STARTED FLAGGING

BEATEN IN THE SPRINT

LET TEAMMATE WIN

DNF

DNS

BLUE PETER BADGE

JUST OUTSIDE THE MEDALS

SPORTIVE FINISHER'S MEDAL

LONE BREAKAWAY CAUGHT 100M FROM LINE

UNDER-ESTIMATED FINAL CLIMB

BRONZE SWIMMING MEDAL

DIDN'T HAVE THE LEGS

MY FREE HOUR

THERE IS JUST ENOUGH TIME TO GO OUT ON THE BIKE

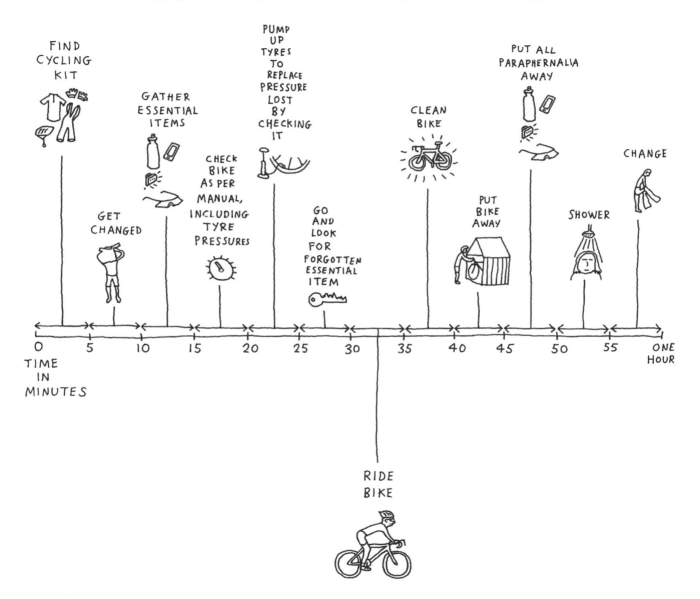

FIND CYCLING KIT

GET CHANGED

GATHER ESSENTIAL ITEMS

CHECK BIKE AS PER MANUAL, INCLUDING TYRE PRESSURES

PUMP UP TYRES TO REPLACE PRESSURE LOST BY CHECKING IT

GO AND LOOK FOR FORGOTTEN ESSENTIAL ITEM

CLEAN BIKE

PUT BIKE AWAY

PUT ALL PARAPHERNALIA AWAY

SHOWER

CHANGE

0   5   10   15   20   25   30   35   40   45   50   55   ONE HOUR

TIME IN MINUTES

RIDE BIKE

MY REGULAR ROUTE

DIAGRAM SHOWING GRADIENTS, HEADWINDS, AND ANGRY DOGS

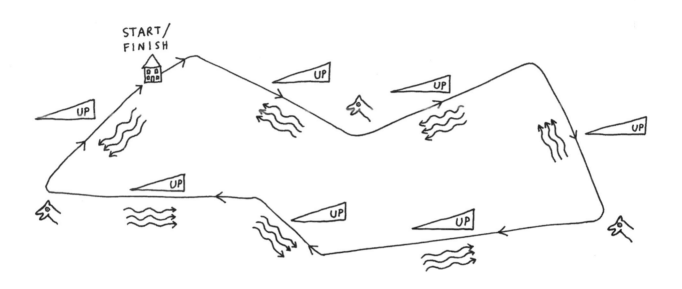

START/
FINISH

KEY

WIND
DIRECTION:

GRADIENT
(UPHILL): UP

DOG
(ANGRY):

GRADIENT
(DOWNHILL): DOWN

CYCLING UPHILL

LEVELS OF SEVERITY

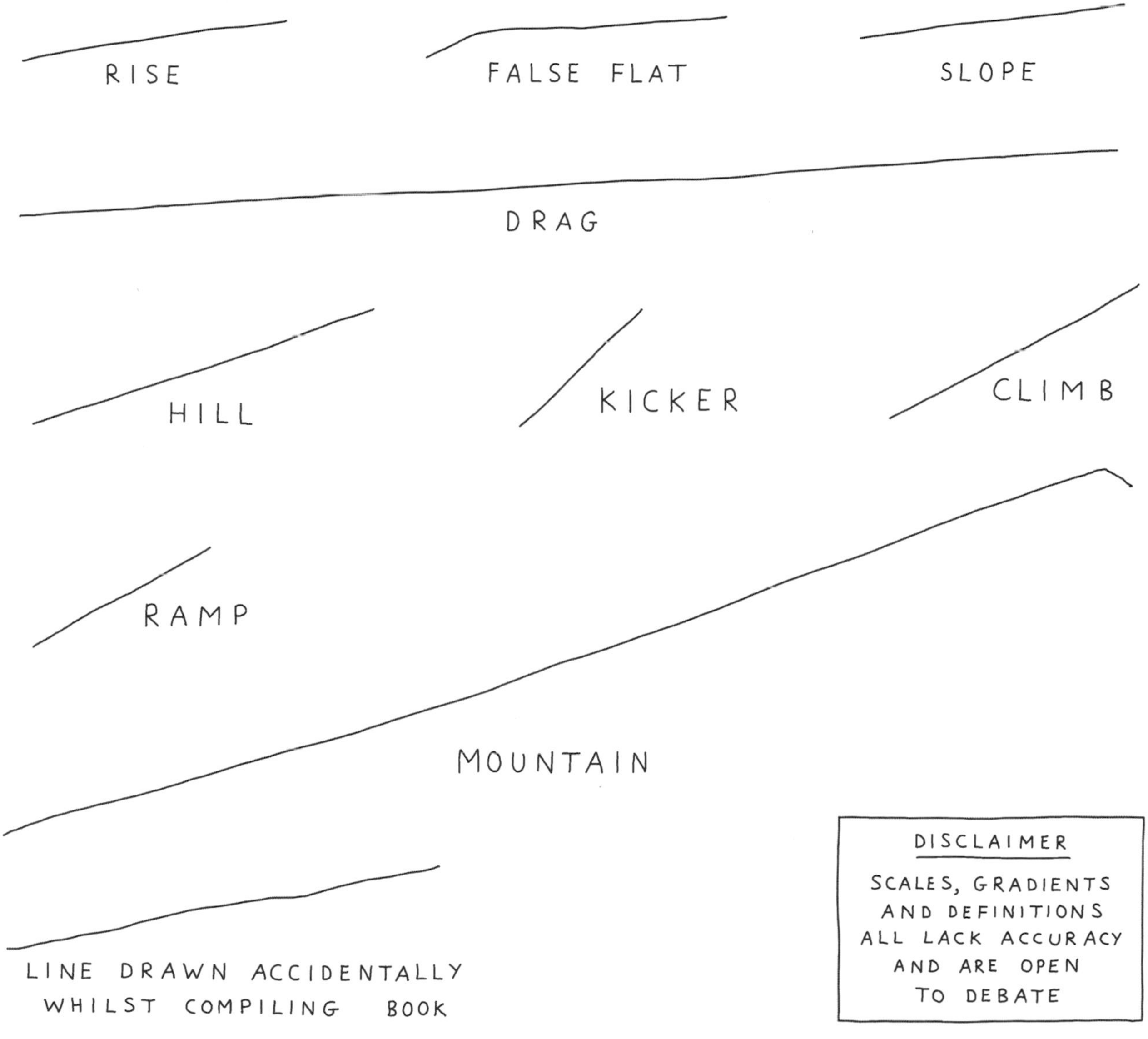
RISE
FALSE FLAT
SLOPE
DRAG
HILL
KICKER
CLIMB
RAMP
MOUNTAIN
LINE DRAWN ACCIDENTALLY WHILST COMPILING BOOK
DISCLAIMER
SCALES, GRADIENTS AND DEFINITIONS ALL LACK ACCURACY AND ARE OPEN TO DEBATE

YOUR COMPONENTS

HOW MUCH THEY COST

WHEN YOU
BOUGHT THEM
AT THE
BICYCLE
SHOP

WHEN ASKED
BY YOUR
FRIENDS
AT THE
CYCLING
CLUB

WHEN ASKED
BY YOUR
PARTNER
AT HOME

UPGRADES

TO MAKE YOU GO FASTER

WHEELS

LIGHTER
AND MORE
AERODYNAMIC

TYRES

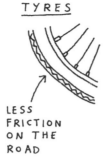

LESS
FRICTION
ON THE
ROAD

GROUPSET

COMPONENTS THAT
WORK BETTER
(AND SHINE MORE)

PEDALS

CLIPLESS.
TRANSFER MORE
POWER (AND MAKE
A NICE 'CLICK')

SADDLE

LOOKS FASTER
TO ME

KIT

POINTIER
HAT

CUTS THROUGH
THE AIR

BAR
TAPE

GO-FASTER STRIPES
(OR OTHER PATTERN)

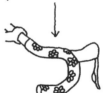

GRADIENT

GO
DOWNHILL
MORE

MEANS
OF
PROPULSION

ROCKET

RIDER

SOMEONE
A BIT
FASTER

BICYCLE COMPONENTS

THEY GET EVERYWHERE

ON THE HANDLEBARS

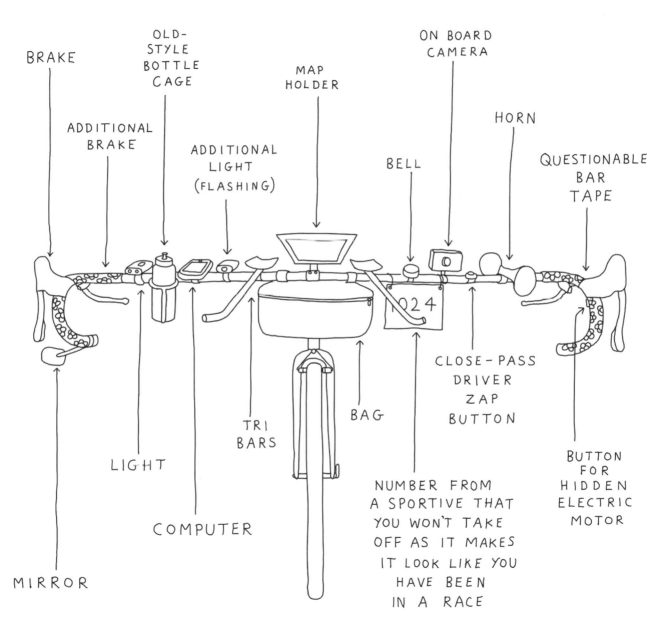

BRAKE

OLD-STYLE BOTTLE CAGE

ON BOARD CAMERA

ADDITIONAL BRAKE

MAP HOLDER

HORN

ADDITIONAL LIGHT (FLASHING)

BELL

QUESTIONABLE BAR TAPE

TRI BARS

BAG

CLOSE-PASS DRIVER ZAP BUTTON

LIGHT

COMPUTER

NUMBER FROM A SPORTIVE THAT YOU WON'T TAKE OFF AS IT MAKES IT LOOK LIKE YOU HAVE BEEN IN A RACE

BUTTON FOR HIDDEN ELECTRIC MOTOR

MIRROR

LIGHTS

RATED AND REVIEWED

BATTERY LIGHT ✳✳✳✳

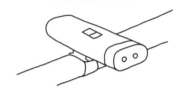

+ BATTERIES EASY TO FIND
− NOT THE BRIGHTEST

RECHARGEABLE LIGHT ✳✳✳✳✳

+ BRIGHT, DOESN'T WEIGH MUCH
− PLACES TO PLUG IN A USB
  SCARCE WHEN OUT RIDING

DYNAMO LIGHT ✳✳✳

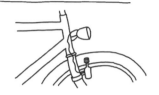

+ YESTERDAY'S TECHNOLOGY
  STILL SEEMS TO WORK
− STOPS WHEN YOU DO

LARGE FLASHLIGHT ✳✳✳

+ A MILLION LUMENS
− BIT BULKY

CHEAP LIGHT THAT EVERYONE SWEARS BY ON FORUMS ✳✳

+ VERY GOOD VALUE
− WERE THE WORKERS PAID?

PHONE TORCH ✳

SHADOWY FIGURE

+ IDEAL FOR FINDING
  YOUR BIKE IN THE SHED
− WILL USE UP YOUR BATTERY

WIND-UP TORCH ✳

+ ECO-FRIENDLY
− DON'T WIND IT ON DESCENTS

CAMPING LIGHT ✳

+ YOU'VE PROBABLY GOT
  ONE IN THE SHED
− GENERALLY UNSUITABLE

TEA LIGHT ✳

+ IDEAL FOR THOSE ON A BUDGET
− OUR SAMPLE REGULARLY
  BLEW OUT ABOVE 2KPH

BELLS AND HORNS

WAYS TO ALERT PEDESTRIANS WHO ARE UNWITTINGLY IN THE WAY

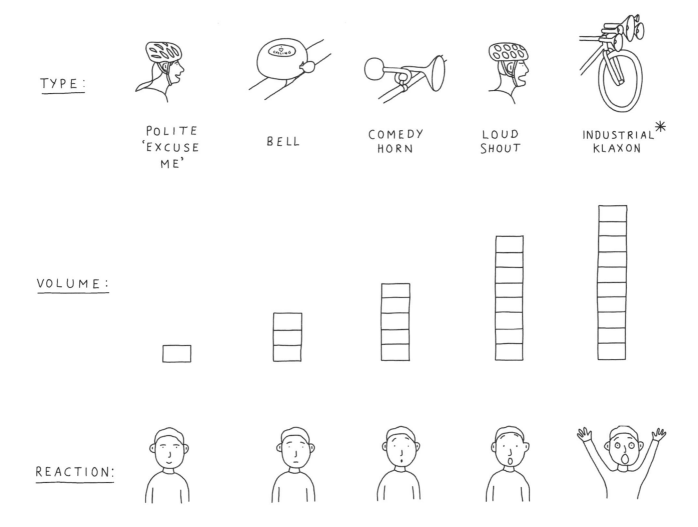

TYPE:

POLITE 'EXCUSE ME'   BELL   COMEDY HORN   LOUD SHOUT   INDUSTRIAL KLAXON *

VOLUME:

REACTION:

*BUT STILL WHAT YOU NEED FOR A DRIVER WHO HASN'T SEEN YOU

THE CYCLING COMPUTER

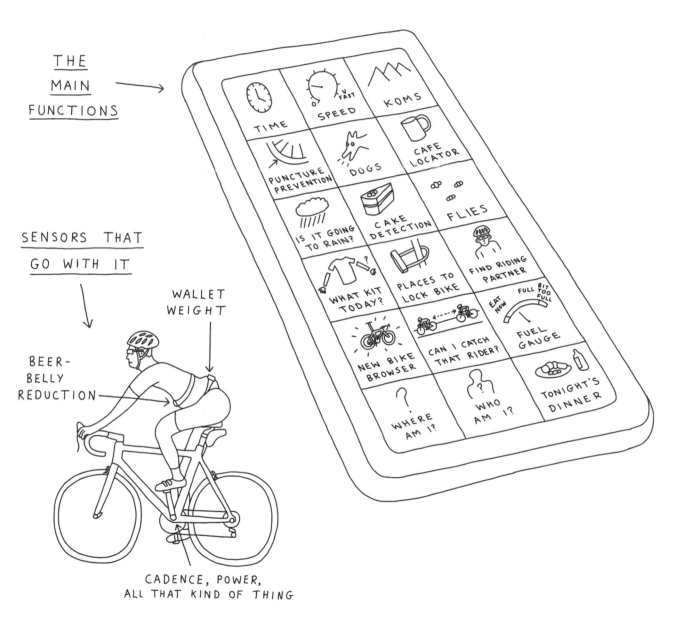

THE MAIN FUNCTIONS

SENSORS THAT GO WITH IT

BEER-BELLY REDUCTION

WALLET WEIGHT

CADENCE, POWER, ALL THAT KIND OF THING

TIME

SPEED

KOMS

PUNCTURE PREVENTION

DOGS

CAFE LOCATOR

IS IT GOING TO RAIN?

CAKE DETECTION

FLIES

WHAT KIT TODAY?

PLACES TO LOCK BIKE

FIND RIDING PARTNER

NEW BIKE BROWSER

CAN I CATCH THAT RIDER?

FUEL GAUGE

EAT NOW · FULL · BIT TOO FULL

WHERE AM I?

WHO AM I?

TONIGHT'S DINNER

THE SADDLE BAG

WHAT'S INSIDE?

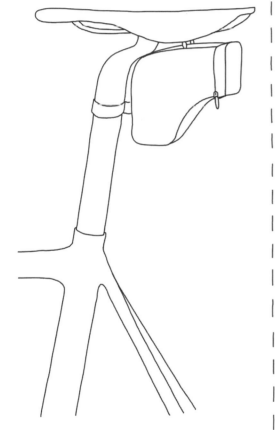

INNER TUBE WITH (HOPEFULLY) CORRECT VALVE

TYRE LEVERS, AND A PUNCTURE REPAIR KIT OF YESTERYEAR

MINI PUMP

FORGOTTEN BANANA

PHONE TO CALL FOR A LIFT HOME

COMB (HELMET HAIR)

ARM WARMERS (YELLOW - THERE WAS A SALE)

EMERGENCY FOOD

MULTI-TOOL (BOTTLE OPENER, ETC)

RAIN JACKET

FOREIGN CURRENCY FROM RECENT CAMPING TRIP

ALLEN KEY

ATTRACTIVE FEATHER PICKED UP FROM ROAD

UNMENDED HOLEY INNER TUBE FROM LAST TIME

MONEY FOR A PINT

TIE (JUST IN CASE)

ALAN'S KEY

NAIL THAT WAS ONCE IN TYRE, KEPT FOR BRAGGING PURPOSES AT CAFE STOPS

A PLASTIC BAG, BECAUSE YOU NEVER KNOW

GOING OUT ON THE BIKE

ACTUALLY USEFUL CHECKLIST OF THINGS YOU MIGHT NEED

 ☐ BOTTLE

 ☐ NAVIGATIONAL DEVICE

 ☐ HELMET

 ☐ GLASSES

 ☐ HAT

 ☐ EXTRA LAYER: WATERPROOF, GILET, ETC

 ☐ SOMETHING TO EAT

 ☐ HOUSE KEY

 ☐ LOCK

 ☐ LIGHTS

 ☐ SPARE INNER TUBE

 ☐ PHONE FOR EMERGENCIES

 ☐ CAFE MONEY

 ☐ MITTS

 ☐ PUMP

 ☐ MULTI-TOOL

 ☐ OVERSHOES (IF WET/COLD)

 ☐ ARM WARMERS

PEDALS

THE DIFFERENT KINDS

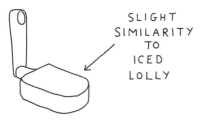

SLIGHT SIMILARITY TO ICED LOLLY

PLATFORM, OR FLAT

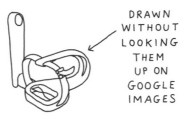

DRAWN WITHOUT LOOKING THEM UP ON GOOGLE IMAGES

CAGE, OR TOE CLIPS

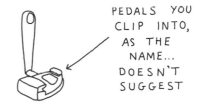

PEDALS YOU CLIP INTO, AS THE NAME... DOESN'T SUGGEST

CLIPLESS

HOW TO USE CLIPLESS PEDALS

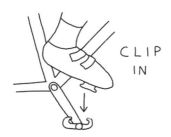

CLIP IN

SEEN FROM ABOVE

CLIP OUT

TWIST

WADDLE AROUND

PRACTISE FALLING OFF
IN DIFFERENT SITUATIONS

AT JUNCTIONS

AT TRAFFIC LIGHTS

ON HILLS

MUDGUARDS

WHO HAS THEM?

NO

YES

NO

YES
(BUT NOT YET FITTED THEM)

NO
(BUT IT HASN'T BEEN RAINING)

YES

NO

YES
(BUT OWNS A DOTTY SHIRT)

YES
(BUT FORGOT TO PUT LID ON BLENDER)

THAT ANNOYING NOISE

POSSIBLE CAUSES OF RATTLES, CLICKS, AND SQUEAKS

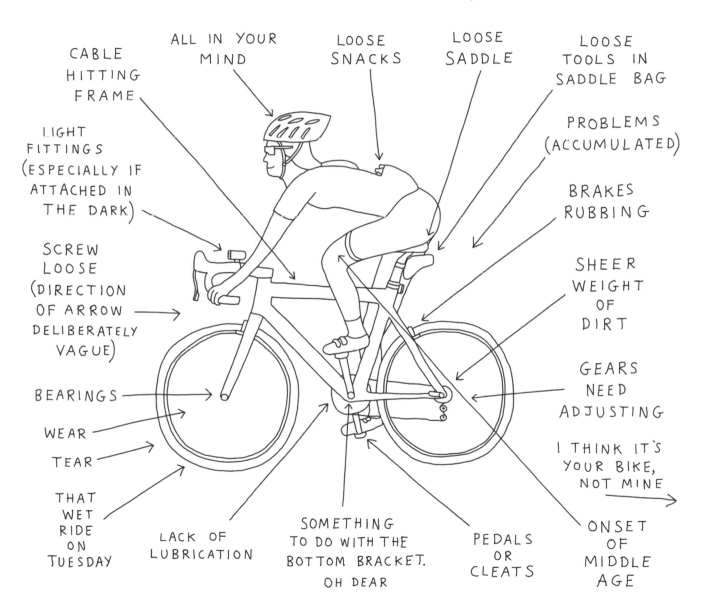

CABLE HITTING FRAME

ALL IN YOUR MIND

LOOSE SNACKS

LOOSE SADDLE

LOOSE TOOLS IN SADDLE BAG

LIGHT FITTINGS (ESPECIALLY IF ATTACHED IN THE DARK)

PROBLEMS (ACCUMULATED)

BRAKES RUBBING

SCREW LOOSE (DIRECTION OF ARROW DELIBERATELY VAGUE)

SHEER WEIGHT OF DIRT

BEARINGS

GEARS NEED ADJUSTING

WEAR

TEAR

I THINK IT'S YOUR BIKE, NOT MINE

THAT WET RIDE ON TUESDAY

LACK OF LUBRICATION

SOMETHING TO DO WITH THE BOTTOM BRACKET. OH DEAR

PEDALS OR CLEATS

ONSET OF MIDDLE AGE

PRE-RIDE CHECKS

QUICK-RELEASES
DONE UP

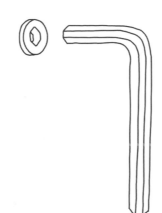

ALL NUTS AND
BOLTS TIGHT

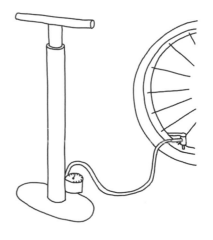

TYRES AT CORRECT
PRESSURE

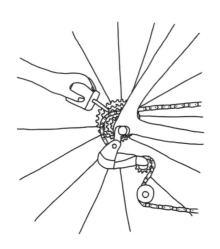

CHAIN LUBED

BRAKES WORK

PARTNER READY TO PICK
YOU UP IN THE CAR

BICYCLE MAINTENANCE

THE ESSENTIAL TOOL KIT

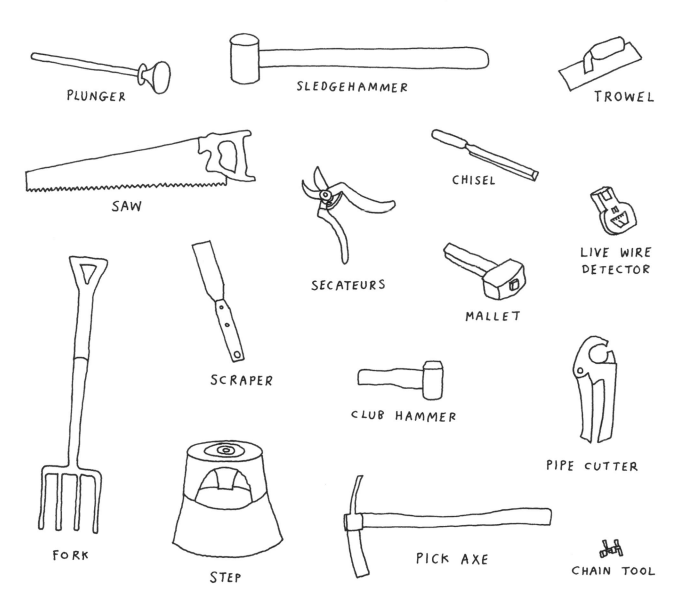

PLUNGER

SLEDGEHAMMER

TROWEL

SAW

SECATEURS

CHISEL

LIVE WIRE DETECTOR

MALLET

SCRAPER

CLUB HAMMER

PIPE CUTTER

FORK

STEP

PICK AXE

CHAIN TOOL

THE SERVICE COURSE

IN MY GARAGE

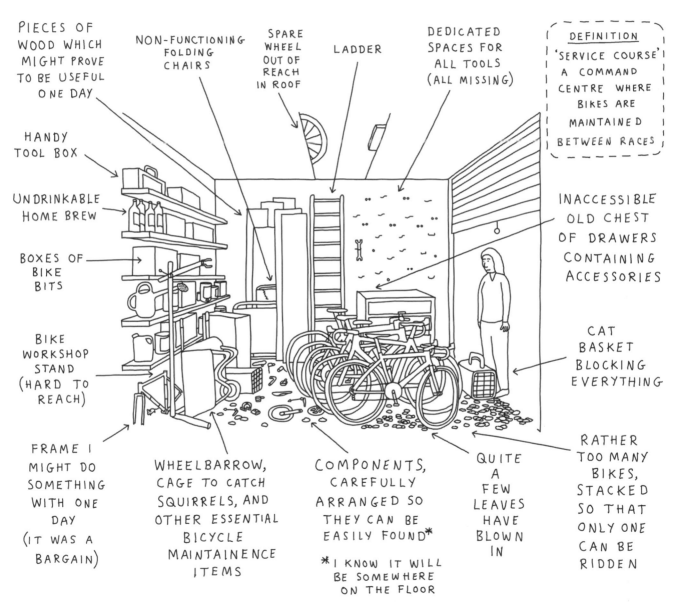

PIECES OF WOOD WHICH MIGHT PROVE TO BE USEFUL ONE DAY

NON-FUNCTIONING FOLDING CHAIRS

SPARE WHEEL OUT OF REACH IN ROOF

LADDER

DEDICATED SPACES FOR ALL TOOLS (ALL MISSING)

DEFINITION
'SERVICE COURSE'
A COMMAND CENTRE WHERE BIKES ARE MAINTAINED BETWEEN RACES

HANDY TOOL BOX

UNDRINKABLE HOME BREW

BOXES OF BIKE BITS

BIKE WORKSHOP STAND (HARD TO REACH)

INACCESSIBLE OLD CHEST OF DRAWERS CONTAINING ACCESSORIES

CAT BASKET BLOCKING EVERYTHING

FRAME I MIGHT DO SOMETHING WITH ONE DAY (IT WAS A BARGAIN)

WHEELBARROW, CAGE TO CATCH SQUIRRELS, AND OTHER ESSENTIAL BICYCLE MAINTAINENCE ITEMS

COMPONENTS, CAREFULLY ARRANGED SO THEY CAN BE EASILY FOUND*

* I KNOW IT WILL BE SOMEWHERE ON THE FLOOR

QUITE A FEW LEAVES HAVE BLOWN IN

RATHER TOO MANY BIKES, STACKED SO THAT ONLY ONE CAN BE RIDDEN

LEVELS OF FURY

WITH A BIKE YOU CAN'T FIX

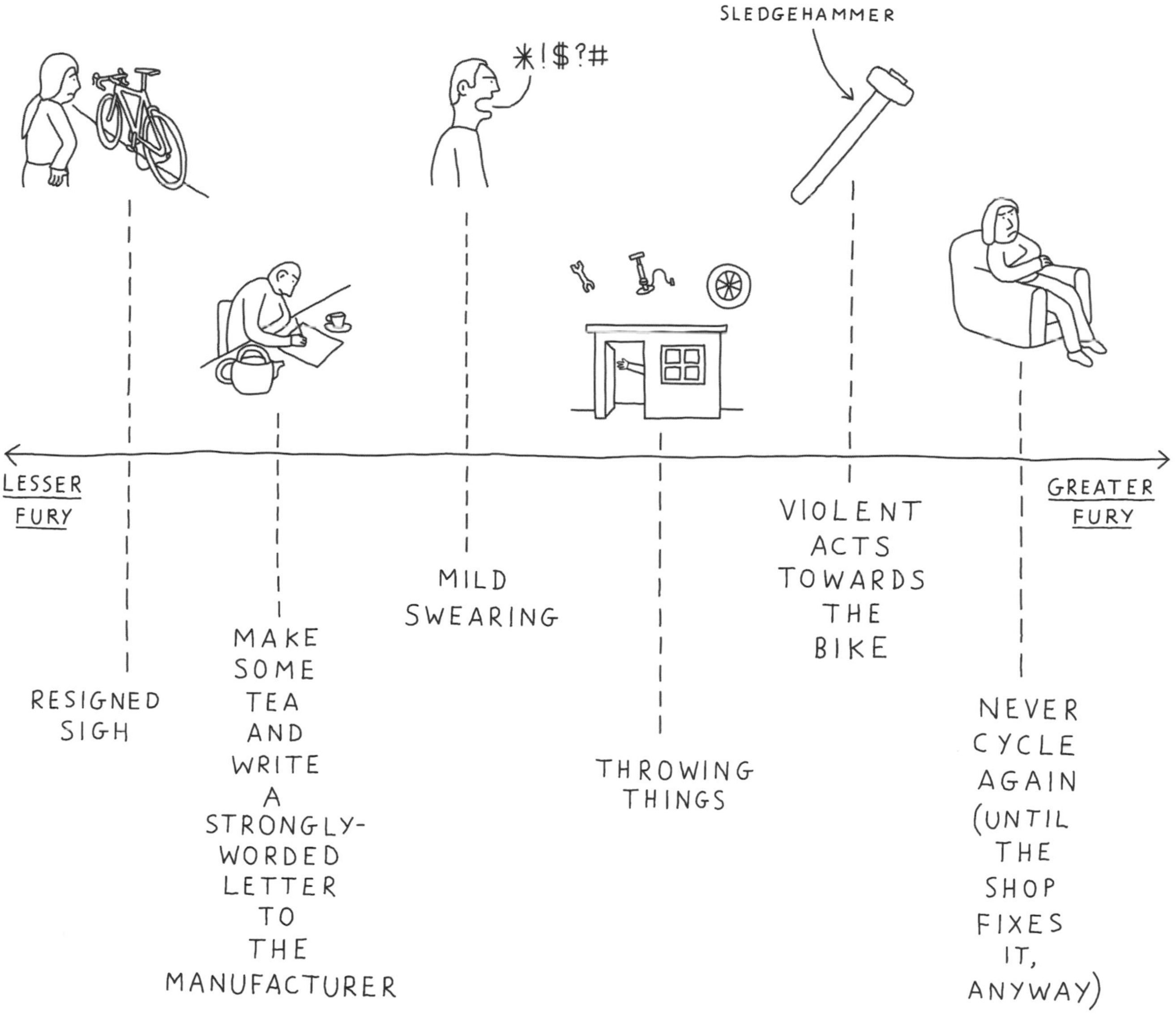
SLEDGEHAMMER
*!$?#
LESSER FURY
GREATER FURY
RESIGNED SIGH
MAKE SOME TEA AND WRITE A STRONGLY-WORDED LETTER TO THE MANUFACTURER
MILD SWEARING
THROWING THINGS
VIOLENT ACTS TOWARDS THE BIKE
NEVER CYCLE AGAIN (UNTIL THE SHOP FIXES IT, ANYWAY)

DISC BRAKES

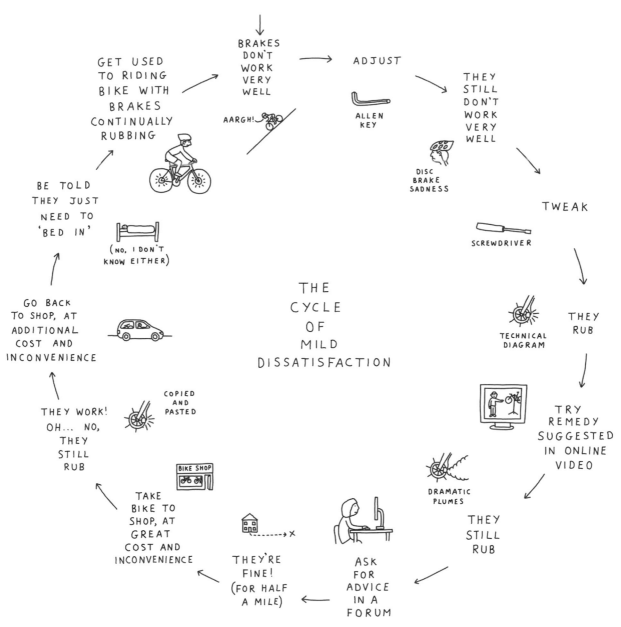

BRAKES DON'T WORK VERY WELL

AARGH!

GET USED TO RIDING BIKE WITH BRAKES CONTINUALLY RUBBING

ADJUST

ALLEN KEY

THEY STILL DON'T WORK VERY WELL

DISC BRAKE SADNESS

BE TOLD THEY JUST NEED TO 'BED IN'

(NO, I DON'T KNOW EITHER)

TWEAK

SCREWDRIVER

THE CYCLE OF MILD DISSATISFACTION

GO BACK TO SHOP, AT ADDITIONAL COST AND INCONVENIENCE

THEY RUB

TECHNICAL DIAGRAM

THEY WORK! OH... NO, THEY STILL RUB

COPIED AND PASTED

TRY REMEDY SUGGESTED IN ONLINE VIDEO

TAKE BIKE TO SHOP, AT GREAT COST AND INCONVENIENCE

BIKE SHOP

DRAMATIC PLUMES

THEY STILL RUB

THEY'RE FINE! (FOR HALF A MILE)

ASK FOR ADVICE IN A FORUM

CHEAP BIKES

FROM THE SUPERMARKET

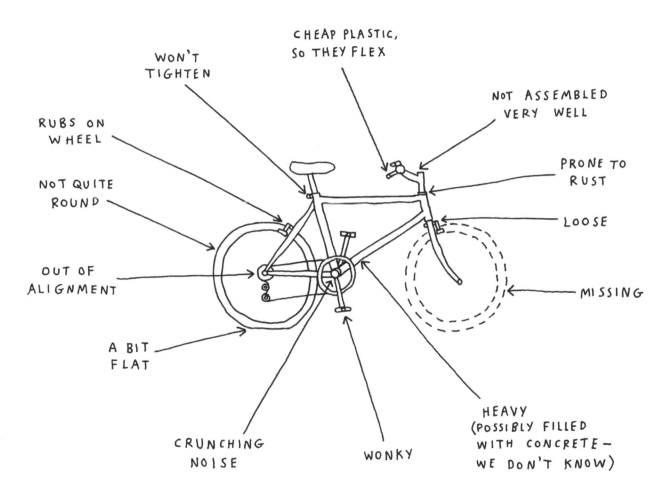

CHEAP PLASTIC,
SO THEY FLEX

WON'T
TIGHTEN

NOT ASSEMBLED
VERY WELL

RUBS ON
WHEEL

PRONE TO
RUST

NOT QUITE
ROUND

LOOSE

OUT OF
ALIGNMENT

MISSING

A BIT
FLAT

CRUNCHING
NOISE

WONKY

HEAVY
(POSSIBLY FILLED
WITH CONCRETE —
WE DON'T KNOW)

APART FROM THIS THEY ARE OK

MENDING A PUNCTURE

WHAT TO DO WHEN YOU ARE OUT ON THE ROAD

OH *$!@#

1 ALERT RIDING COMPANIONS, THEN STOP

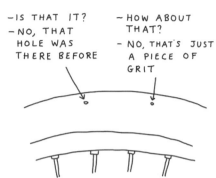

- IS THAT IT?
- NO, THAT HOLE WAS THERE BEFORE
- HOW ABOUT THAT?
- NO, THAT'S JUST A PIECE OF GRIT

2 EXAMINE TYRE FOR ANY GREAT BIG THORNS OR NAILS

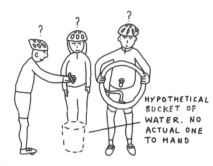

HYPOTHETICAL BUCKET OF WATER. NO ACTUAL ONE TO HAND

3 TRY THE THING WITH THE LEVERS AND THE PATCHES AND THE GLUE AND THE SANDPAPER AND THE CHALK AND THE BUCKET OF WATER

4 SEE WHETHER ANYONE HAS AN INNER TUBE

5 TRY EVERYONE'S MINI-PUMP TO SEE WHETHER THERE IS ONE THAT ACTUALLY WORKS

COULD YOU COME AND PICK ME UP?

NO. I'M IN A WARM HOUSE, WATCHING CSI

6 PHONE YOUR PARTNER, WHO IS IN A WARM HOUSE, WATCHING CSI, AND ASK FOR A LIFT

PUNCTURES

WAYS TO AVOID THEM

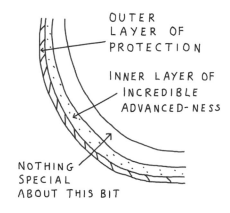

OUTER LAYER OF PROTECTION

INNER LAYER OF INCREDIBLE ADVANCED-NESS

NOTHING SPECIAL ABOUT THIS BIT

BUY EXPENSIVE TYRES WITH ADDED PROTECTION

TYRE GOO

FILL TYRES WITH SLIME / SAND*/CONCRETE*

*NOT TRIED

CARPET FREQUENTLY-USED ROUTES

STOP AND CARRY BIKE IF A SHARD OF GLASS IS SEEN

EMPLOY A SWEEPER TO WALK AHEAD

[YOUR BRILLIANT IDEA HERE]

CLEANING YOUR BIKE

IT IS A BIT OF A CHORE

TRY TO FIND
CLEANING EQUIPMENT

CHISEL OFF LARGER
PIECES OF MUD

ATTEMPT TO UNTANGLE
THE HOSE

SHAMPOO

SOAK THE WHEELS

DEGREASE

SCRUB

FETCH YET ANOTHER
BUCKET OF WATER

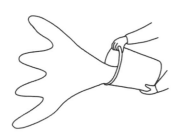

RINSE

DO THE BITS
YOU MISSED

POLISH

LUBRICATE

TRAINING ADVICE

WISDOM GAINED BY READING SEVERAL MAGAZINE ARTICLES

GET THE MILES IN
DURING THE OFF-SEASON

CUT OUT LOTS OF
TASTY FOODS

EVERY NOW AND THEN
GO ABSOLUTELY FLAT OUT

DO THIS DAY
AFTER DAY
AFTER DAY
AFTER DAY...

(WELL, WITH AN
OCCASIONAL
DAY OFF)

YOU WILL
ALMOST
CERTAINLY
WIN

UNLESS
YOU
COMPETE
AGAINST
SOMEONE
WHO
CUT OUT
EVEN
MORE
TASTY
FOODS

OR
SOMEONE
WHO
COULD
AFFORD
TO
TRAIN
IN
MAJORCA
FOR
SEVERAL
WEEKS

OR
SOMEONE
WHO
IS
JUST
SLIGHTLY
MORE
NATURALLY
GIFTED
THAN
YOU

FINISH

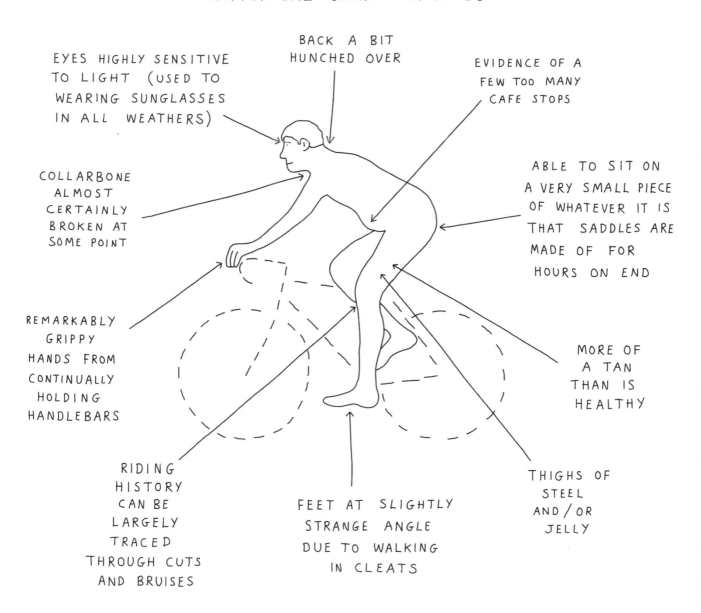

THE CYCLIST

ANATOMICAL CHARACTERISTICS

EYES HIGHLY SENSITIVE TO LIGHT (USED TO WEARING SUNGLASSES IN ALL WEATHERS)

BACK A BIT HUNCHED OVER

EVIDENCE OF A FEW TOO MANY CAFE STOPS

COLLARBONE ALMOST CERTAINLY BROKEN AT SOME POINT

ABLE TO SIT ON A VERY SMALL PIECE OF WHATEVER IT IS THAT SADDLES ARE MADE OF FOR HOURS ON END

REMARKABLY GRIPPY HANDS FROM CONTINUALLY HOLDING HANDLEBARS

MORE OF A TAN THAN IS HEALTHY

RIDING HISTORY CAN BE LARGELY TRACED THROUGH CUTS AND BRUISES

FEET AT SLIGHTLY STRANGE ANGLE DUE TO WALKING IN CLEATS

THIGHS OF STEEL AND/OR JELLY

SHAVED LEGS

WHY DO CYCLISTS SHAVE THEIR LEGS? REASONS I HAVE HEARD:

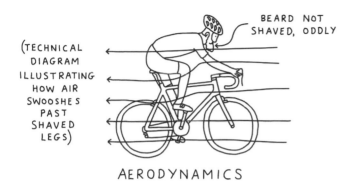

(TECHNICAL DIAGRAM ILLUSTRATING HOW AIR SWOOSHES PAST SHAVED LEGS)

BEARD NOT SHAVED, ODDLY

AERODYNAMICS

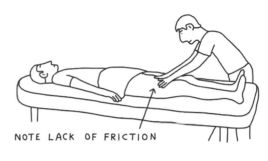

NOTE LACK OF FRICTION

IT MAKES MASSAGES EASIER

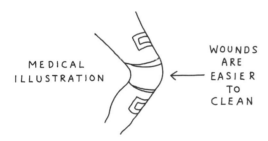

MEDICAL ILLUSTRATION

WOUNDS ARE EASIER TO CLEAN

IT DOESN'T HURT SO MUCH WHEN YOU FALL OFF

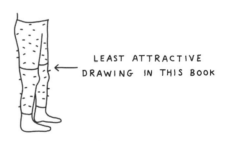

LEAST ATTRACTIVE DRAWING IN THIS BOOK

IT STOPS HAIRS POKING THROUGH LYCRA

THE TRUTH:

WE HAVE SEEN PROS WITH THEIR LEGS SHAVED AND WANT TO BE A BIT LIKE THEM

THE TURBO TRAINER
SIMULATING ACTUAL CYCLING CONDITIONS

BARKING DOGS

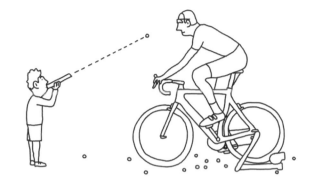

STONES AND BEES

RAIN

HILLS

MINOR CYCLING INJURIES

STUNG BY NETTLE
ON NARROW PATH

BANGED KNEE ON CROSSBAR
WHILST AVOIDING SMALL STONE

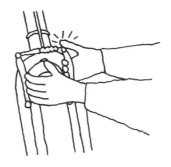

TRAPPED THUMB TRYING
TO ADJUST BRAKES

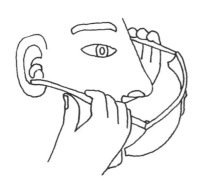

POKED EAR WHEN
PUTTING ON SUNGLASSES

BUMPED ELBOW CLOSING
GARAGE DOOR

SQUASHED TOE OVERTIGHTENING
VELCRO ON SHOES

#MINORCYCLINGINJURIES

TRAINING
LEVELS OF INTENSITY

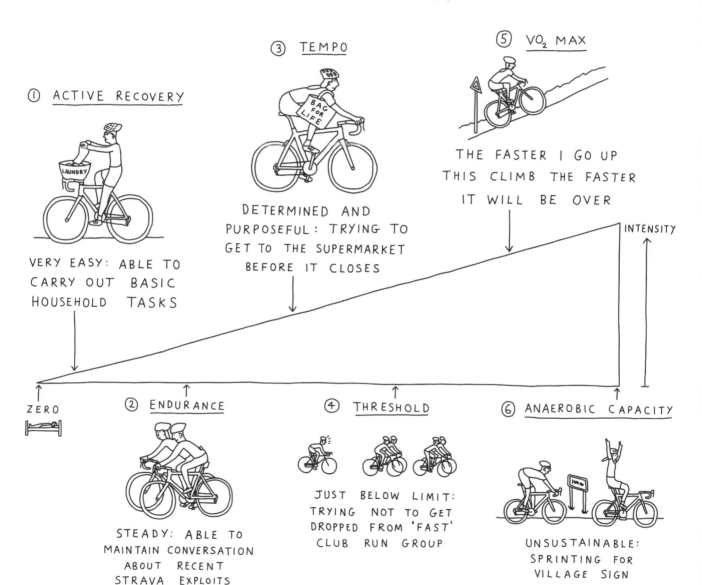

① ACTIVE RECOVERY

VERY EASY: ABLE TO CARRY OUT BASIC HOUSEHOLD TASKS

③ TEMPO

DETERMINED AND PURPOSEFUL: TRYING TO GET TO THE SUPERMARKET BEFORE IT CLOSES

⑤ VO₂ MAX

THE FASTER I GO UP THIS CLIMB THE FASTER IT WILL BE OVER

INTENSITY

ZERO

② ENDURANCE

STEADY: ABLE TO MAINTAIN CONVERSATION ABOUT RECENT STRAVA EXPLOITS

④ THRESHOLD

JUST BELOW LIMIT: TRYING NOT TO GET DROPPED FROM 'FAST' CLUB RUN GROUP

⑥ ANAEROBIC CAPACITY

UNSUSTAINABLE: SPRINTING FOR VILLAGE SIGN

IN THE MUSETTE

WHAT IS THERE?

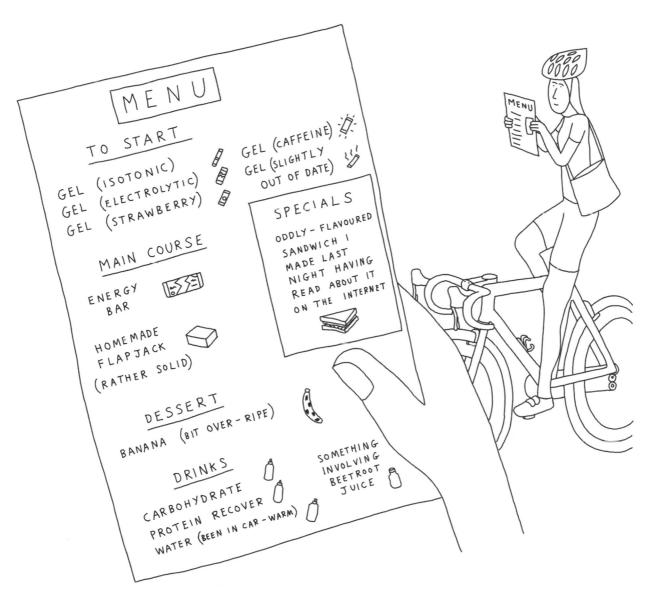

MENU

TO START

GEL (ISOTONIC)
GEL (ELECTROLYTIC)
GEL (STRAWBERRY)
GEL (CAFFEINE)
GEL (SLIGHTLY OUT OF DATE)

MAIN COURSE

ENERGY BAR

HOMEMADE FLAPJACK (RATHER SOLID)

SPECIALS

ODDLY-FLAVOURED SANDWICH I MADE LAST NIGHT HAVING READ ABOUT IT ON THE INTERNET

DESSERT

BANANA (BIT OVER-RIPE)

DRINKS

CARBOHYDRATE
PROTEIN RECOVER
WATER (BEEN IN CAR - WARM)

SOMETHING INVOLVING BEETROOT JUICE

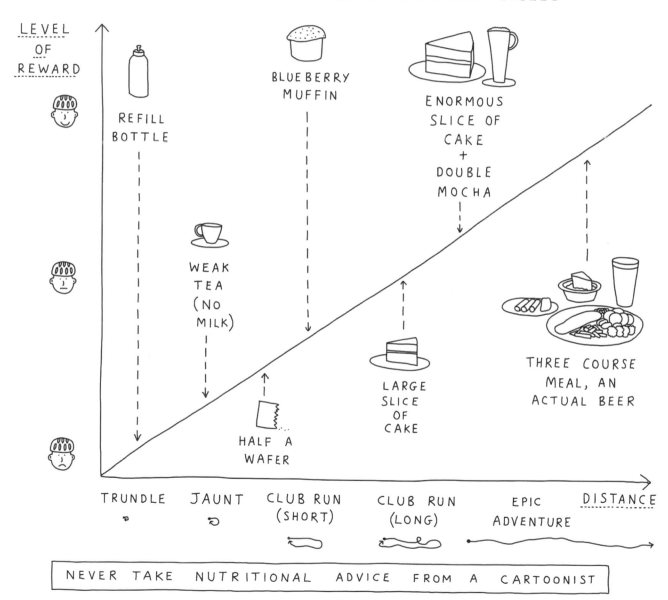

REWARDS

AT THE CAFE DEPENDS UPON DISTANCE CYCLED

LEVEL OF REWARD

REFILL BOTTLE

BLUEBERRY MUFFIN

ENORMOUS SLICE OF CAKE + DOUBLE MOCHA

WEAK TEA (NO MILK)

HALF A WAFER

LARGE SLICE OF CAKE

THREE COURSE MEAL, AN ACTUAL BEER

TRUNDLE JAUNT CLUB RUN (SHORT) CLUB RUN (LONG) EPIC ADVENTURE

DISTANCE

NEVER TAKE NUTRITIONAL ADVICE FROM A CARTOONIST

HYDRATION

IT IS IMPORTANT

SCIENTIFIC DIAGRAM
SHOWING WATER
CIRCULATING
AROUND THE
BODY OF
A HUMAN
CYCLIST

PERILS OF EXCESSIVE HYDRATION

SINGLE
PORTALOO

VALID

YOUR
TEAM CAR

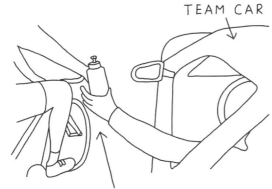

THE 'STICKY BOTTLE'.
(POSSIBLY NOT ENTIRELY VALID)

INVALID

EXCESSIVE PRE-LOADING
OF LIQUID
THE NIGHT BEFORE

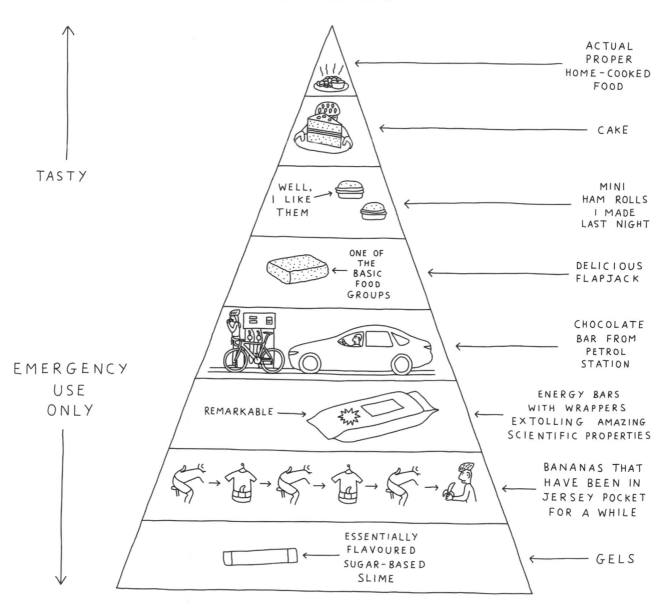

ENERGY SNACKS

THE HIERARCHY

TASTY

EMERGENCY USE ONLY

ACTUAL PROPER HOME-COOKED FOOD

CAKE

WELL, I LIKE THEM

MINI HAM ROLLS I MADE LAST NIGHT

ONE OF THE BASIC FOOD GROUPS

DELICIOUS FLAPJACK

CHOCOLATE BAR FROM PETROL STATION

REMARKABLE

ENERGY BARS WITH WRAPPERS EXTOLLING AMAZING SCIENTIFIC PROPERTIES

BANANAS THAT HAVE BEEN IN JERSEY POCKET FOR A WHILE

ESSENTIALLY FLAVOURED SUGAR-BASED SLIME

GELS

CYCLING CLOTHING

THE DIFFERENT ITEMS AND WHAT THEY MEAN

SHORTS

MY NEED TO BE COMFORTABLE
OUTWEIGHS ANY SENSE
OF EMBARRASSMENT

CAP

TRYING TO KEEP RAIN/
SUN OUT OF EYES IN
A NOSTALGIC MANNER

TRADE TEAM JERSEY

BEING A MOBILE BILLBOARD
IS A PRICE WORTH PAYING TO
SUPPORT MY FAVOURITE TEAM

MITTS

MY HANDS GET SORE, AND
IT IS ENTIRELY POSSIBLE
THAT I MAY FALL OFF

OVERSHOES

I GET COLD FEET, AND AM
HAPPY TO STRUGGLE FOR TEN
MINUTES PULLING THESE ON

KNEE WARMERS

IT'S A BIT CHILLY.
I THINK. IS IT?
I'M NOT SURE

LYCRA

FINE	HAVE ANOTHER LOOK IN THE WARDROBE
TRAINING 	DOING THE WEEKLY SHOP 
WINNING 	AT A DRINKS RECEPTION 
SITTING AROUND, SHOWING OFF 	IN A RESTAURANT 

THE CYCLING HELMET

CROSS-SECTION

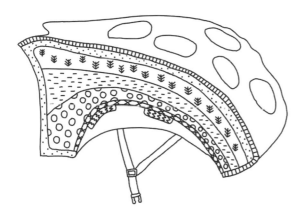

	HARD PLASTIC SHELL
	POLYSTYRENE
	FEATHERS
	CUSTARD
	THE RUBBER THEY MAKE THOSE REALLY BOUNCY RUBBER BALLS OUT OF
	SWEAT-PROOF MEMBRANE
	SPONGY BITS (VELCROED ON, AND USUALLY IN NEED OF A WASH)

ALL ARGUMENTS ABOUT HELMETS TO BE CONFINED WITHIN THIS BOX

TYPES

HAIR NET

ACCEPTABLE IN THE 80S →

VENTED

COOLS YOU DOWN
SLOWS YOU DOWN →

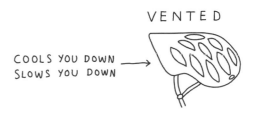

AERO

HEATS YOU UP
SPEEDS YOU UP →

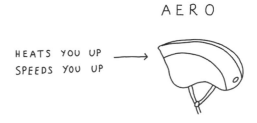

TIME TRIAL

POINTY →

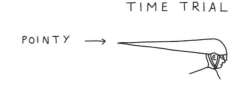

BIB SHORTS

|

MISPLACED
STRAPS

BACK TO FRONT

REVERSE THE
MANOUVRE

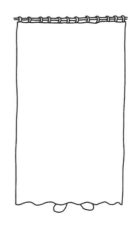

HIDE IN A
CUBICLE

MISPLACED
LIMBS

GENERALLY IN
A TANGLE

CARRY ON AND PRETEND
THAT NOTHING IS AMISS

ALARM

ONLY TO BE
USED IN CASE
OF BIB-SHORT
EMERGENCIES

PANIC

GLOVES
DIFFERENT SORTS

MITTS

THEY OFTEN HAVE THE CORRECT NUMBER OF DIGITS. BUT FIGURES IN THESE DIAGRAMS TEND ONLY TO HAVE THREE FINGERS

VELCRO FASTENING

MITTENS

ON STRING. FOR THE RIDER WHO TENDS TO LOSE THEIRS EASILY

WINTER GLOVES

SOMETIMES THEY ONLY HAVE TWO FINGERS. STICK-ON EYES OPTIONAL

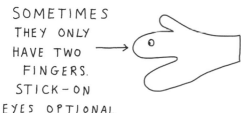

OVEN MITTS

NO CYCLING PURPOSE. FOR COOKING YOUR DINNER WHEN YOU GET HOME

NO GLOVES AT ALL

PROS, PEOPLE PRETENDING TO BE PROS, THOSE CONFIDENT THEY WILL NOT FALL OFF, THOSE WITH HOT HANDS

THE GLOVES I LEFT AT HOME AS IT REALLY DIDN'T LOOK AS IF I WOULD NEED THEM

BUT THEN IT TURNED OUT THAT I REALLY DID

MARIGOLDS

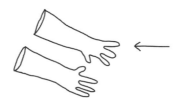

DOING HOUSEHOLD CHORES TO ATONE FOR HAVING BOUGHT A NEW BIKE WITHOUT CONSULTATION

UNDISCOVERED CLOTHING

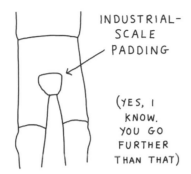

INDUSTRIAL-
SCALE
PADDING

(YES, I
KNOW.
YOU GO
FURTHER
THAN THAT)

SHORTS THAT STILL
FEEL COMFORTABLE
AFTER 86 MILES

OVERSHOES THAT YOU CAN
GET ON AND OFF WITHOUT
TOO MUCH DIFFICULTY

BREATHABLE JACKET
THAT REALLY IS AS GOOD
AS THE ONES PEOPLE GO
ON AND ON ABOUT

TECHNICAL
ILLUSTRATION

WAVES OF
COLD AIR

SHOE

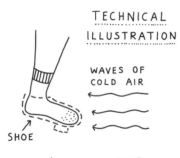

NUMBNESS

'THERMAL' WINTER
SOCKS THAT ACTUALLY
KEEP THE CHILL OUT

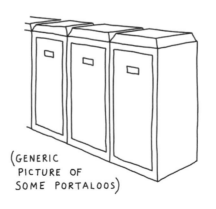

(GENERIC
PICTURE OF
SOME PORTALOOS)

BIB SHORTS THAT DO NOT
MAKE VISITS TO THE LOO
INCREDIBLY COMPLICATED

HAVE YOU SEEN
MY FAVOURITE
JERSEY?

YOUR
FAVOURITE
JERSEY

JOINING A CYCLING CLUB

HOW TO GO ABOUT IT

DO SOME RESEARCH
ON THE INTERNET

TURN UP FOR A CLUB RUN

DECIDE WHETHER
YOU COULD LIVE
WITH THE CLUB KIT

GO TO
A CLUB
NIGHT
AND
LOOK
LOST →

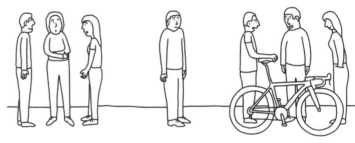

VOLUNTEER FOR
SOMETHING

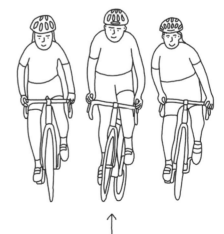

HAVE A BRILLIANT TIME

75

THE CLUB RUN

THERE ARE SEVERAL GROUPS

FAST

SEGMENTS

OCCASIONAL CHAT
ABOUT AERO WHEELS

SPRINTING FOR SIGNS

INTERMEDIATE

WISH THEY WERE
IN THE FAST
GROUP, BUT KNOW
THEY WOULDN'T
KEEP UP

SLOW

TEA, CAKE,
CHAT, CAKE

ANYONE SEEN
BRIAN?

TODAY'S ROUTE

WHERE ARE WE GOING?

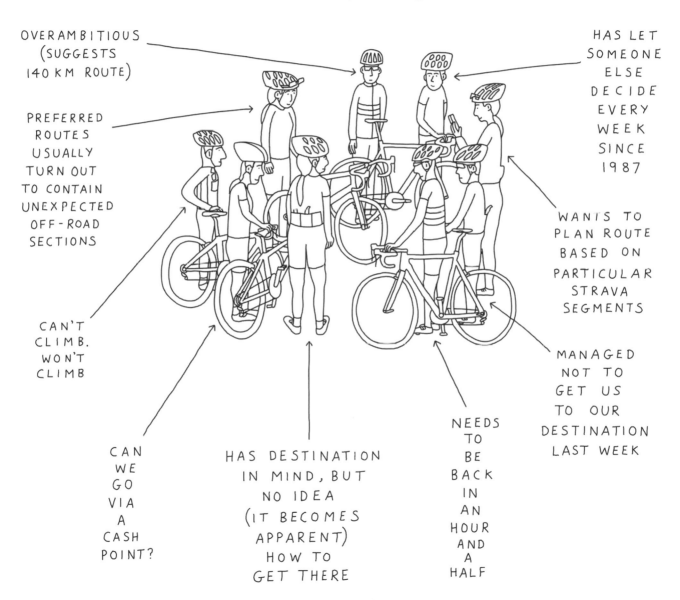

OVERAMBITIOUS
(SUGGESTS
140 KM ROUTE)

HAS LET
SOMEONE
ELSE
DECIDE
EVERY
WEEK
SINCE
1987

PREFERRED
ROUTES
USUALLY
TURN OUT
TO CONTAIN
UNEXPECTED
OFF-ROAD
SECTIONS

WANTS TO
PLAN ROUTE
BASED ON
PARTICULAR
STRAVA
SEGMENTS

CAN'T
CLIMB.
WON'T
CLIMB

MANAGED
NOT TO
GET US
TO OUR
DESTINATION
LAST WEEK

CAN
WE
GO
VIA
A
CASH
POINT?

HAS DESTINATION
IN MIND, BUT
NO IDEA
(IT BECOMES
APPARENT)
HOW TO
GET THERE

NEEDS
TO
BE
BACK
IN
AN
HOUR
AND
A
HALF

PROTECTING YOUR BIKE

WHEN YOU STOP AT A CAFE

1. KEEP A CONTINUAL EYE ON IT

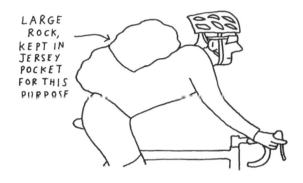

2. LOCK IT TO SOMETHING SOLID

3. LEAVE A STRONGLY-WORDED NOTE

4. REMOVE AN IMPORTANT COMPONENT

THE CYCLING CLUB

THE MEMBERS

SERIOUS COMPETITORS RACE MOST WEEKS

SUNDAY CLUB RUN REGULARS

ONLY REALLY SEEN AT SOCIAL EVENTS

JOINED FOR THE KIT

BELONG BECAUSE SPOUSE DOES

WE NEVER SEE THESE PEOPLE, BUT THEY KEEP PAYING THEIR SUBS

DO ALL OF THE JOBS: COMMITTEE POSTS, MARSHALING, ORGANISING EVENTS, SOCIAL MEDIA, MAKING THE TEA, ETC

JOINED BY ACCIDENT THINKING THIS WAS THE RECYCLING CLUB

RECRUITING VOLUNTEERS

TO MARSHAL THE CLUB '10'

ADVERTISING

GETTING EXISTING VOLUNTEERS TO BRING FRIENDS

TARGETING INDIVIDUALS

MAKING THREATS

BRIBERY

FLATTERY

USING A CARROT

USING A STICK

DECIDE THAT WE DON'T REALLY NEED MARSHALLS ANYWAY

SUNDAY MORNING

YOU WILL SEE CYCLISTS GATHERING ON QUIET COUNTRY LANES

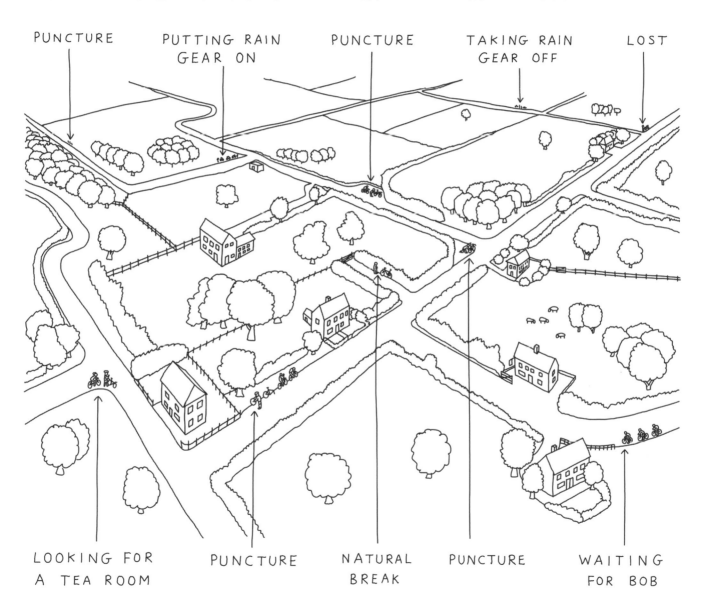

PUNCTURE

PUTTING RAIN GEAR ON

PUNCTURE

TAKING RAIN GEAR OFF

LOST

LOOKING FOR A TEA ROOM

PUNCTURE

NATURAL BREAK

PUNCTURE

WAITING FOR BOB

TURBO TRAINING
A SESSION AT THE CYCLING CLUB

THE CYCLING CAFE

SHINY BIKES ON THE WALL

CAFE PROS (HAVE GOT THE SEAT BY THE RADIATOR)

JERSEY FROM FAMOUS RIDER WHO WAS A REGULAR (POPPED IN ONCE)

BIKE ART

RACING ON TELEVISION

RACING TO GET A GOOD TABLE

RATHER EXPENSIVE COFFEE

LAPTOP-USER WHO HAS BEEN THERE SEVEN HOURS AND BOUGHT ONE DRINK

ROADIES WHO HAVE DONE 90 MILES

ROADIES WHO HAVE DONE 3 MILES (BUT TRYING TO LOOK LIKE THEY HAVE DONE 90)

GREATER PERCENTAGE OF BEARDS AND CYCLING CAPS THAN ONE WOULD FIND AMONG GENERAL POPULATION

THOUSANDS OF POUNDS-WORTH OF UNLOCKED BIKES. FORTUNATELY MINE IS ALWAYS THE LEAST EXPENSIVE

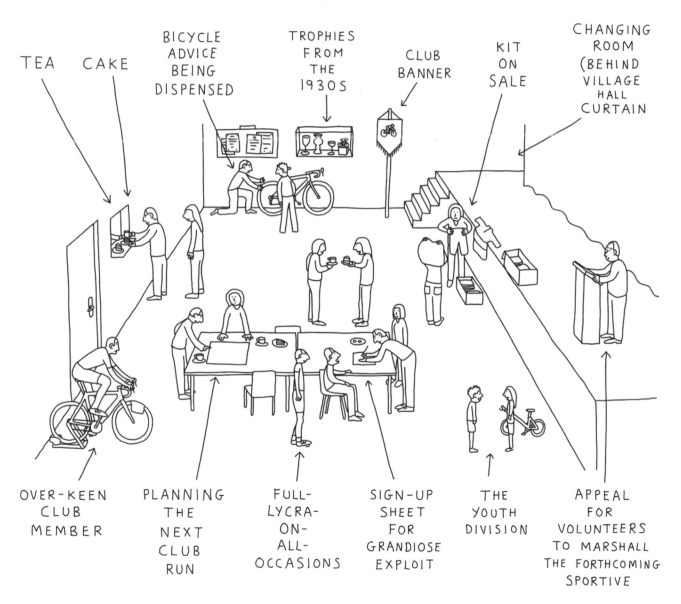

THE CLUB NIGHT
A SOCIAL GATHERING OF THE CYCLING CLUB

TEA

CAKE

BICYCLE ADVICE BEING DISPENSED

TROPHIES FROM THE 1930S

CLUB BANNER

KIT ON SALE

CHANGING ROOM (BEHIND VILLAGE HALL CURTAIN

OVER-KEEN CLUB MEMBER

PLANNING THE NEXT CLUB RUN

FULL-LYCRA-ON-ALL-OCCASIONS

SIGN-UP SHEET FOR GRANDIOSE EXPLOIT

THE YOUTH DIVISION

APPEAL FOR VOLUNTEERS TO MARSHALL THE FORTHCOMING SPORTIVE

THE SUNDAY CLUB RUN

SORRY, I COULDN'T MAKE IT

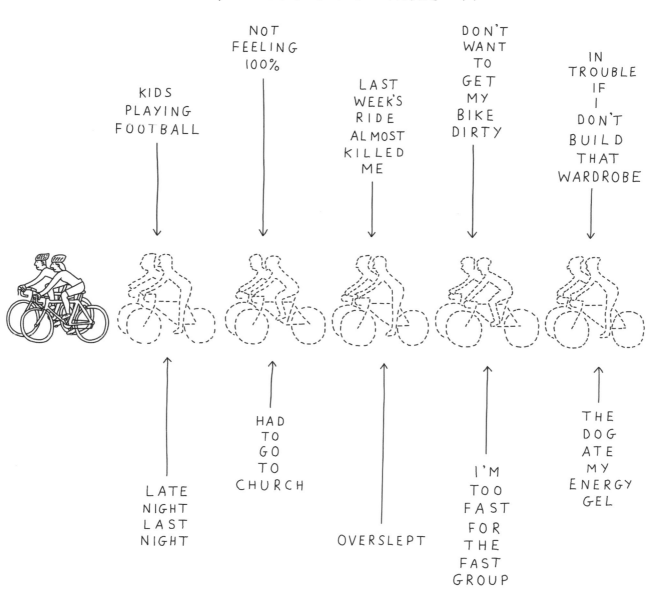

KIDS PLAYING FOOTBALL

NOT FEELING 100%

LAST WEEK'S RIDE ALMOST KILLED ME

DON'T WANT TO GET MY BIKE DIRTY

IN TROUBLE IF I DON'T BUILD THAT WARDROBE

LATE NIGHT LAST NIGHT

HAD TO GO TO CHURCH

OVERSLEPT

I'M TOO FAST FOR THE FAST GROUP

THE DOG ATE MY ENERGY GEL

THIS MORNING'S BIKE RIDE

IT WAS A DISASTER

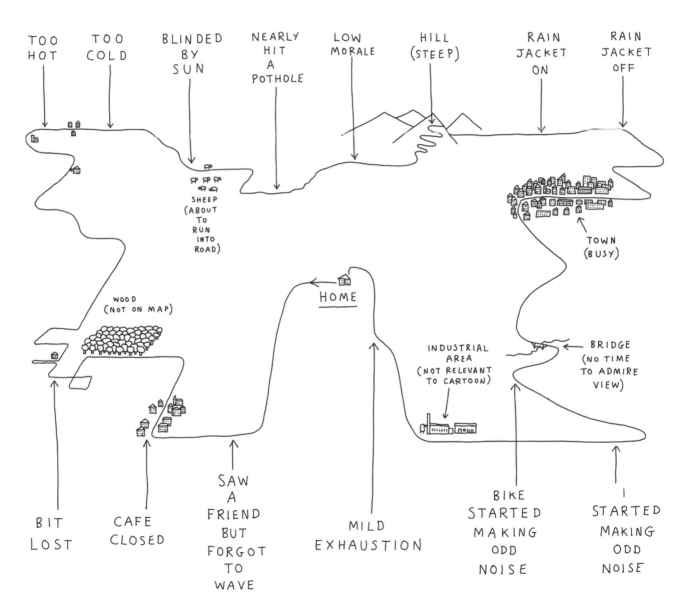

THE CYCLE RACE

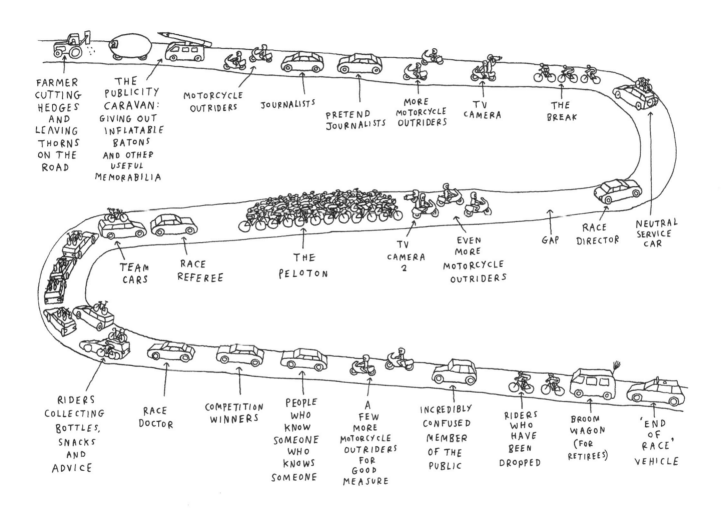

FARMER CUTTING HEDGES AND LEAVING THORNS ON THE ROAD

THE PUBLICITY CARAVAN: GIVING OUT INFLATABLE BATONS AND OTHER USEFUL MEMORABILIA

MOTORCYCLE OUTRIDERS

JOURNALISTS

PRETEND JOURNALISTS

MORE MOTORCYCLE OUTRIDERS

TV CAMERA

THE BREAK

NEUTRAL SERVICE CAR

RACE DIRECTOR

GAP

EVEN MORE MOTORCYCLE OUTRIDERS

TV CAMERA 2

THE PELOTON

RACE REFEREE

TEAM CARS

RIDERS COLLECTING BOTTLES, SNACKS AND ADVICE

RACE DOCTOR

COMPETITION WINNERS

PEOPLE WHO KNOW SOMEONE WHO KNOWS SOMEONE

A FEW MORE MOTORCYCLE OUTRIDERS FOR GOOD MEASURE

INCREDIBLY CONFUSED MEMBER OF THE PUBLIC

RIDERS WHO HAVE BEEN DROPPED

BROOM WAGON (FOR RETIREES)

'END OF RACE' VEHICLE

THE TEAM

THE SPRINTER

THE CLIMBER

THE DOMESTIQUE

THE GC RIDER

THE LEAD-OUT
RIDER

SECRETLY WANTS
TO BE LEADER

SPY FROM
RIVAL TEAM

DISGRACED RIDER
SACKED LAST WEEK

RELATIVE OF
THE MANAGER

MAKING UP
THE NUMBERS

ON WORK
EXPERIENCE

MANAGER
(HAD SOME 2ND
PLACES IN 1987)

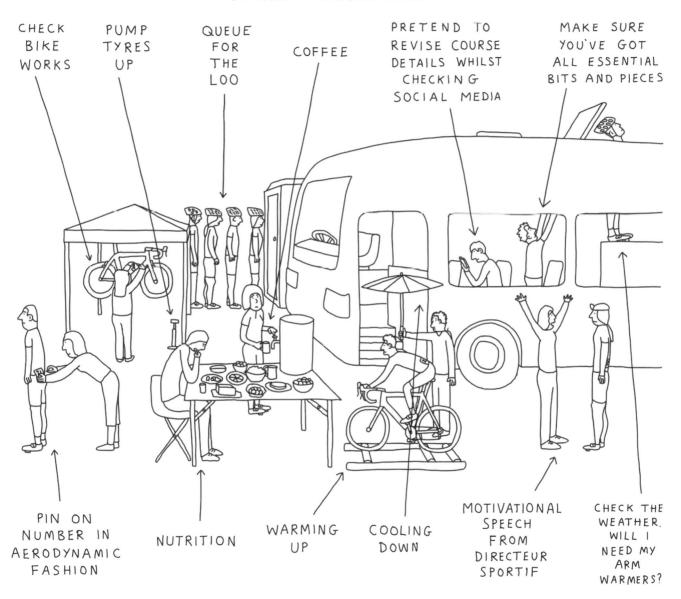

BEFORE A RACE

FINAL PREPARATIONS

CHECK BIKE WORKS

PUMP TYRES UP

QUEUE FOR THE LOO

COFFEE

PRETEND TO REVISE COURSE DETAILS WHILST CHECKING SOCIAL MEDIA

MAKE SURE YOU'VE GOT ALL ESSENTIAL BITS AND PIECES

PIN ON NUMBER IN AERODYNAMIC FASHION

NUTRITION

WARMING UP

COOLING DOWN

MOTIVATIONAL SPEECH FROM DIRECTEUR SPORTIF

CHECK THE WEATHER. WILL I NEED MY ARM WARMERS?

IN THE PELOTON

AREAS TO AVOID

THE FRONT.
HAVE TO DO
ALL THE WORK

THE MIDDLE.
NOWHERE TO
GO IF EVERYONE
SUDDENLY BRAKES

THE BACK.
HAVE TO SPRINT
AFTER EVERY
CORNER

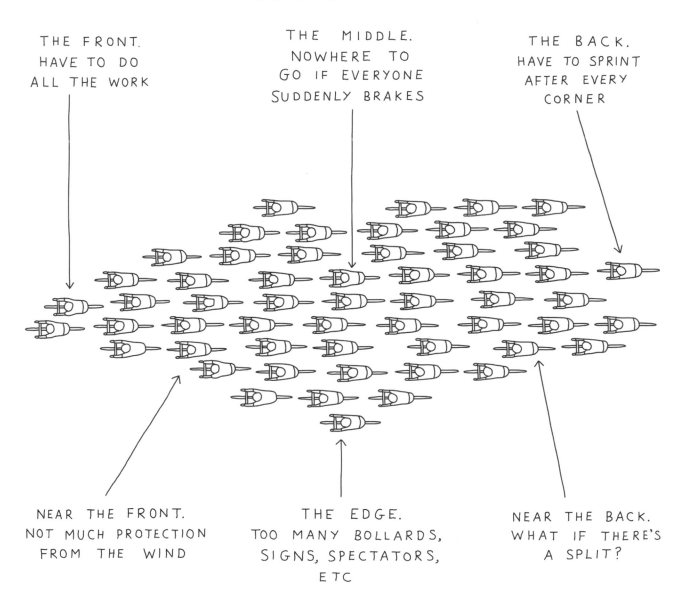

NEAR THE FRONT.
NOT MUCH PROTECTION
FROM THE WIND

THE EDGE.
TOO MANY BOLLARDS,
SIGNS, SPECTATORS,
ETC

NEAR THE BACK.
WHAT IF THERE'S
A SPLIT?

THE CLIMB

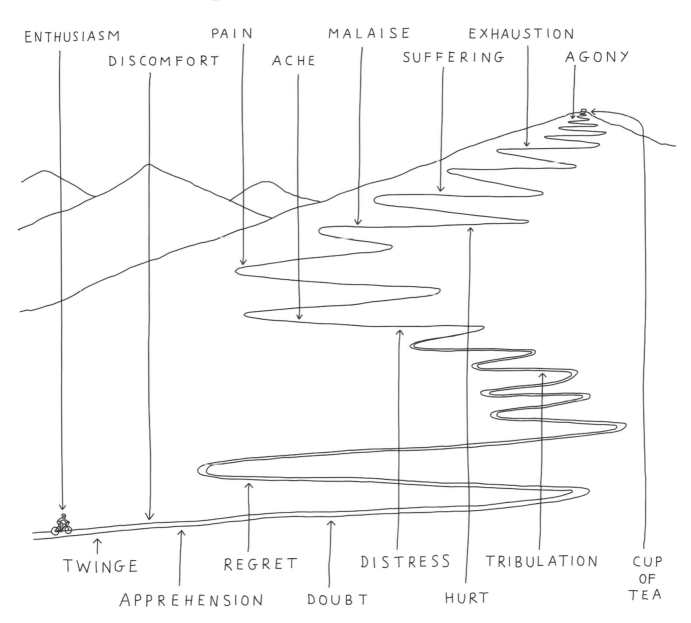

ENTHUSIASM

DISCOMFORT

PAIN

ACHE

MALAISE

SUFFERING

EXHAUSTION

AGONY

TWINGE

APPREHENSION

REGRET

DOUBT

DISTRESS

HURT

TRIBULATION

CUP OF TEA

TACTICS

IN GENERAL

YOU SAVE ENERGY BY RIDING BEHIND SOMEONE ELSE

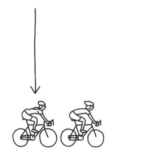

IN THE BUNCH

SAVE YOUR ENERGY

TRY TO BE SOMEWHERE IN HERE

NOT HERE

IN A BREAKAWAY

TRY TO BE HERE MOST OF THE TIME

NOT HERE

(BUT, IF EVERYONE DOES THIS, THE BREAK WON'T STAY AWAY)

CHASING THE BREAKAWAY

TRY TO BE HERE

NOT HERE

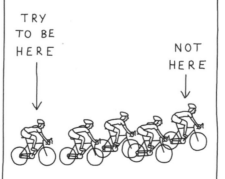

(BUT, IF EVERYONE DOES THIS, THE BREAK WILL STAY AWAY)

AT THE FINISH

TRY TO BE HERE

NOT HERE

FINISH

THE STRAGGLERS

WHAT HAPPENED TO THEM?

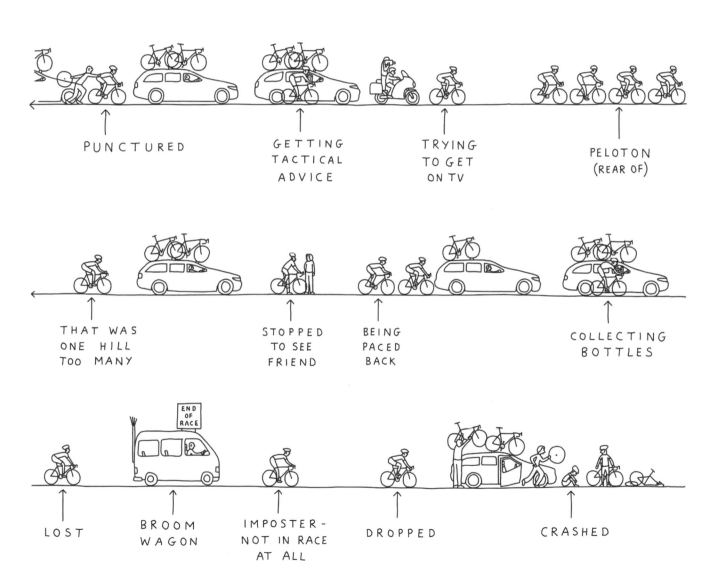

PUNCTURED

GETTING
TACTICAL
ADVICE

TRYING
TO GET
ON TV

PELOTON
(REAR OF)

THAT WAS
ONE HILL
TOO MANY

STOPPED
TO SEE
FRIEND

BEING
PACED
BACK

COLLECTING
BOTTLES

LOST

BROOM
WAGON

IMPOSTER-
NOT IN RACE
AT ALL

DROPPED

CRASHED

COOLING DOWN

COOLING DOWN AFTER A RACE HELPS THE BODY RECOVER

METABOLIC WASTE IS FLUSHED FROM THE MUSCLES

IT CAN BE DONE BY GENTLY SPINNING ON ROLLERS FOR 5 MINUTES

ALSO IT MAKES YOU LOOK LIKE YOU KNOW WHAT YOU ARE DOING

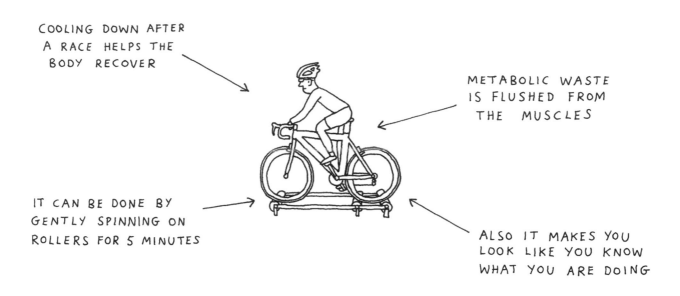

THESE PRINCIPLES CAN ALSO BE OF BENEFIT IN OTHER AREAS OF LIFE

AFTER YOUR WEEKLY SUPERMARKET SHOP

COOL DOWN FOR 5 MINUTES BY PUSHING AN EMPTY TROLLEY AROUND THE CAR PARK

AFTER CATCHING UP WITH A LOT OF EMAILS

COOL DOWN FOR 5 MINUTES BY TYPING SLOWLY AT 1-2 WORDS PER MINUTE

AFTER DRIVING YOUR CAR A LONG DISTANCE

BRRRRRRRRRRRRRRR

COOL DOWN FOR 5 MINUTES BY SITTING IN A CHAIR AND MAKING MOTORING NOISES

GREAT CYCLING MOMENTS

MISSED THROUGH SNOOZING

THE AUDACIOUS ATTACK

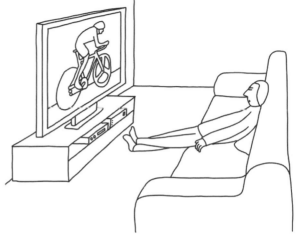

THE REMARKABLE TIME TRIAL

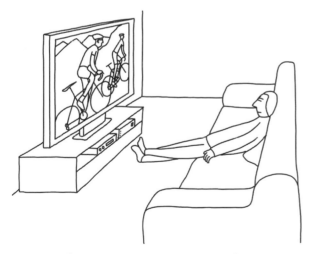

THE MOUNTAIN DUEL

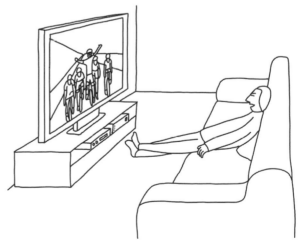

THE INCREDIBLE VICTORY

SPECTATING

AT A BIKE RACE. THESE ARE THE THINGS YOU WILL NEED:

 **RAINCOAT AND SUN LOTION**

 **ENOUGH WATER**

 SOMETHING TO WRITE ON THE ROAD WITH

 MONEY FOR SNACKS/ BEER

 MAP SHOWING DIRECTION OF NEAREST SNACKS/ BEER

 WIG

 GOOD SHOES FOR THE WALK BACK TO YOUR CAR, PARKED SIX MILES AWAY

 **FLAG OF YOUR COUNTRY/TEAM**

 A BOOK TO READ DURING THE THREE HOURS BEFORE ANYTHING HAPPENS

 BAG FOR RACE CARAVAN GIFTS (ONE OF WHICH WILL ALMOST CERTAINLY BE A BAG)

 CAMERA (BUT YOU WILL MISS THE ACTION WHILE YOU TAKE YOUR SHOT)

 SOMETHING FOR AUTOGRAPHS

 **COSTUME**

 LIST OF RIDER NUMBERS (IF YOU CONSULT THIS I WILL BE AMAZED)

 **PICNIC**

 NO, THIS DESIGN PROBABLY WOULDN'T WORK

FOLDING CHAIR

 A HAT YOU CAN TAKE OFF WHEN GIVEN ONE WITH THE SPONSOR'S NAME ON

 UMBRELLA (TO USE AS A ~~SUNSHADE~~ UMBRELLA)

JERSEYS

THAT YOU MAY WELL SPOT WITHIN THE PELOTON

GENERAL
CLASSIFICATION
(SOMETIMES YELLOW)

POINTS
(IMAGINE A VERY VERY
GREEN SHADE OF WHITE)

YOUNG RIDER
(OFTEN WHITE IN
REAL LIFE TOO)

MOUNTAINS

UNSUNG
DOMESTIQUE

MOST
STYLISH

BEARD

LEFT-
HANDED

BEST RECOVERY
FROM LAST NIGHT'S
CELEBRATIONS

BATTLING
THROUGH
ADVERSITY

FLAMBOYANCY
(IRONICALLY, USUALLY
A SHADE OF BEIGE)

PLUCKINESS
(A PARTICULARLY
BRAVE SHADE OF ORANGE)

OH SO
CLOSE

ARMCHAIR
EXPERT

KEEPING UP WITH
BUNCH DESPITE
GREAT AGE

LANTERNE
ROUGE

PLAT DU
JOUR

BEST
IN SHOW

FLORAL JERSEY
(AWARDED
AT RANDOM)

TODAY'S
RAFFLE
WINNER

THE WATER BOTTLE

WE HAVE WAITED HOURS FOR THE RACE

VIEW SEEN BY THE PERSON
WHO WATCHES THE EXCITING
SPECTACLE AS IT SPEEDS PAST

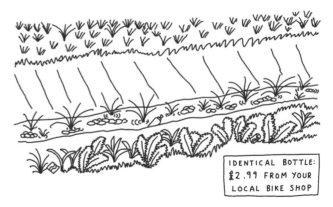

IDENTICAL BOTTLE:
£2.99 FROM YOUR
LOCAL BIKE SHOP

VIEW SEEN BY THE PERSON WHO
GOES TO RETREIVE A RIDER'S
WATER BOTTLE FROM A DITCH

THE TOUR CARAVAN

FREE GIFTS ARE THROWN FROM UNUSUAL VEHICLES TO WAITING SPECTATORS

STRATEGIES FOR RICH PICKINGS

BRING FRIENDS AND POSITION THEM AT INTERVALS ALONG THE ROAD

STAND YOUR GROUND

NO ONE TAKES A FREE GIFT FROM A SMALL CHILD

USE AN UMBRELLA

OR A NET

PROFOUND SUGGESTION FOR RACEGOERS

WHY NOT SHARE?

THOUGHT FOR BIKE-RACE SPONSORS

NON-RECYCLABLE GIANT FOAM HAND

PLASTIC NOVELTY SPECTACLES

DO WE REALLY NEED THIS MANY THROWAWAY KNICK-KNACKS AND THIS MUCH WASTE?

THE TOUR DE FRANCE

HOW TO GO AND WATCH IT

DOWNLOAD A MAP AND TRY TO DECIDE UPON A VIEWING SPOT

ARRIVE EARLY, CARRYING EVERYTHING YOU WILL NEED

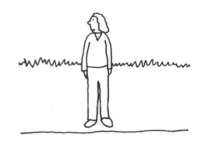

WAIT

FIGHT FELLOW SPECTATORS FOR A SMALL PAPER FLAG THROWN FROM THE PUBLICITY CARAVAN

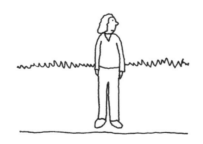

WAIT A BIT LONGER

HOPE THAT, WHEN THE RACE FINALLY ARRIVES, YOUR VIEW ISN'T OBSCURED BY A MAN RUNNING ALONGSIDE THE RIDERS DRESSED AS A GIANT SPRIG OF BROCCOLI

THE TEAM CAR

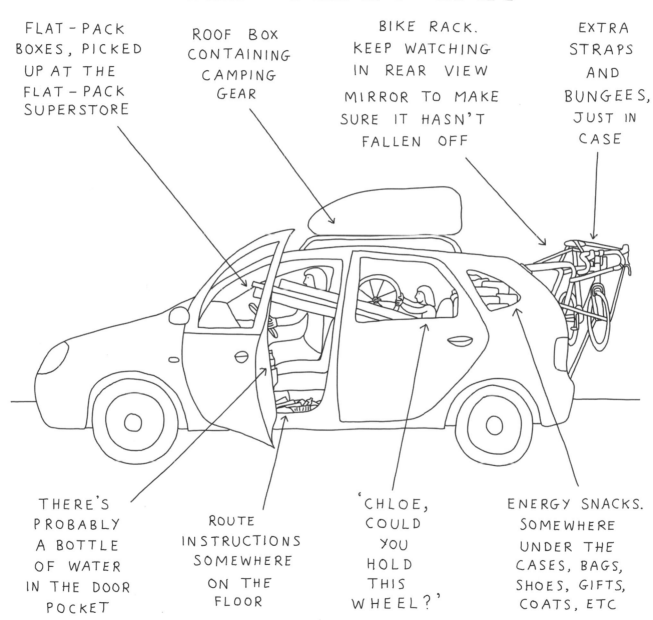

FLAT-PACK BOXES, PICKED UP AT THE FLAT-PACK SUPERSTORE

ROOF BOX CONTAINING CAMPING GEAR

BIKE RACK. KEEP WATCHING IN REAR VIEW MIRROR TO MAKE SURE IT HASN'T FALLEN OFF

EXTRA STRAPS AND BUNGEES, JUST IN CASE

THERE'S PROBABLY A BOTTLE OF WATER IN THE DOOR POCKET

ROUTE INSTRUCTIONS SOMEWHERE ON THE FLOOR

'CHLOE, COULD YOU HOLD THIS WHEEL?'

ENERGY SNACKS. SOMEWHERE UNDER THE CASES, BAGS, SHOES, GIFTS, COATS, ETC

THE RACE CONVOY

LESSER-KNOWN VEHICLES

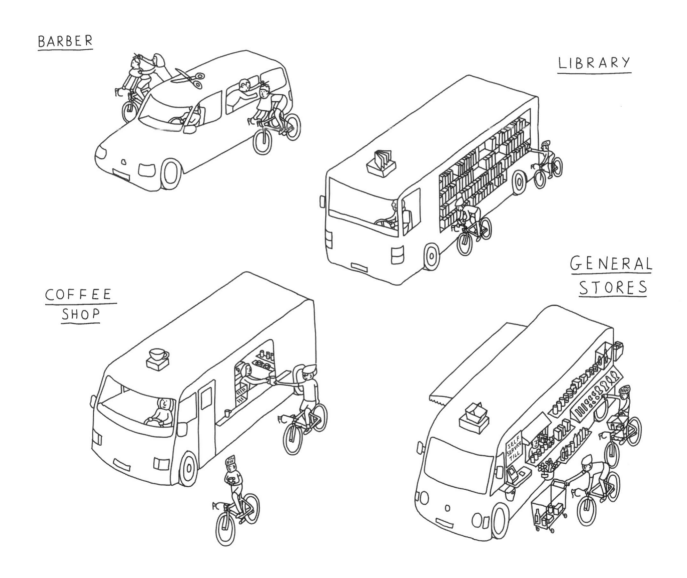

BARBER

LIBRARY

COFFEE SHOP

GENERAL STORES

RACE MARSHALS

THEIR ROLES

STANDING IN THE
RAIN, POINTING
THE WAY

EXPLAINING TO PEOPLE
WHY THEY CAN'T
CROSS AT THE MOMENT

GUARDING
THE
BARRIERS

RACE
MARSHAL

(YOU'LL
HAVE
TO
TAKE
MY
WORD
FOR IT)

WEARING
FLOURESCENT
KIT

THERE
REALLY IS A
BICYCLE RACE
COMING, SO
YOU'LL HAVE TO
STOP I'M
AFRAID

STOPPING
THE
TRAFFIC

HOT
WATER
BOTTLE

TEA

HEATER

TRYING
TO
RECOVER

CHEATING

IN A BIKE RACE

DRUGS

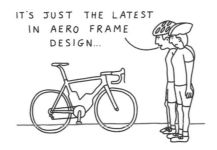

IT'S JUST THE LATEST IN AERO FRAME DESIGN...

HIDDEN MOTORS

HANGING ON TO TEAM CAR

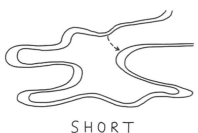

SHORT CUTS

SABOTAGE

JUDGE'S COMPUTER WITH THE RESULTS ON

CYCLING CYBERCRIME

GETTING A LIFT

HIDING BEHIND A TREE FOR ONE LAP

TRAINING AND TRAINING AND TRAINING UNTIL YOU'RE BETTER THAN ANYONE ELSE

CYCLING TACTICS

OBSERVED IN EVERYDAY LIFE

DRAFTING

SKILFUL DESCENDING

BRIDGING TO THE BREAK

PUB

THE FEED ZONE

BIT AND BIT

AS DEMONSTRATED BY GRANNIES DOING THEIR WEEKLY RUN TO THE SHOPS

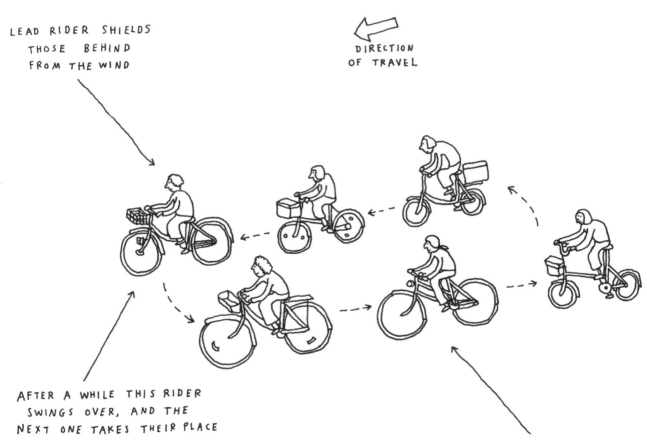

LEAD RIDER SHIELDS THOSE BEHIND FROM THE WIND

DIRECTION OF TRAVEL

AFTER A WHILE THIS RIDER SWINGS OVER, AND THE NEXT ONE TAKES THEIR PLACE

THESE RIDERS ARE SHELTERED BY THE ONES IN FRONT, SO CAN REST UNTIL IT IS THEIR TURN AT THE FRONT AGAIN

THE COBBLED CLASSICS

WAYS TO PREPARE

PRACTISE RESISTING DISTRACTIONS

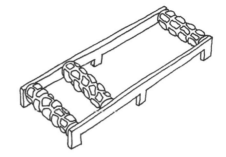

TRAIN ON COBBLED ROLLERS

PREPARE FOR ALL WEATHERS

GET USED TO GRIPPING
THE HANDLEBARS

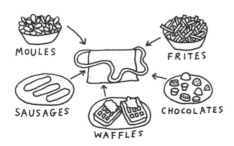

FILL THE MUSETTES

REHEARSE LIFTING THE
VICTORY COBBLE

MARGINAL GAINS

HOW THE PROFESSIONALS MAKE SMALL CHANGES TO IMPROVE THEIR PERFORMANCE

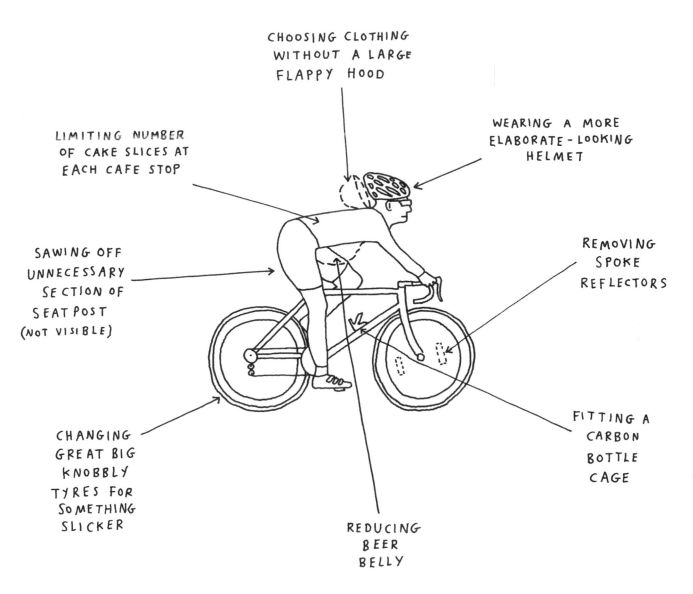

CHOOSING CLOTHING WITHOUT A LARGE FLAPPY HOOD

WEARING A MORE ELABORATE-LOOKING HELMET

LIMITING NUMBER OF CAKE SLICES AT EACH CAFE STOP

SAWING OFF UNNECESSARY SECTION OF SEAT POST (NOT VISIBLE)

REMOVING SPOKE REFLECTORS

CHANGING GREAT BIG KNOBBLY TYRES FOR SOMETHING SLICKER

FITTING A CARBON BOTTLE CAGE

REDUCING BEER BELLY

THINGS CYCLISTS CARRY

ACCORDING TO CYCLING COMMENTATORS

SPADE
(TO ALLOW THEM
TO DIG DEEP)

(NOTE THAT THEY
RETAIN THEIR
CLIPLESS PROPERTIES)

SPECIAL SHOES
(TO HELP THEM
DANCE ON THE PEDALS)

PROTECTIVE
GLASSES
(IN CASE OTHER RIDERS
BLOW UP)

REAR VIEW MIRROR
(FOR SAFETY, IF THEY
START GOING
BACKWARDS ON
A CLIMB)

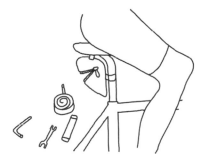

UNZIPPED
SADDLE BAG
(SO THEY CAN LEAVE
EVERYTHING ON
THE ROAD)

A BASIC
SEWING KIT
(TO BE USED
WHEN THE
ELASTIC SNAPS)

CYCLING COMMENTATORS

SKILLS REQUIRED

SHARING A TINY
COMMENTARY BOX
WITH CO-PRESENTER

ACCEPTANCE
OF LIMITED
DINING OPTIONS

ABILITY TO TALK
ABOUT VERY LITTLE FOR
HOURS ON SLOW DAYS

NOT PANICKING
WHEN THE TECHNOLOGY
BREAKS DOWN

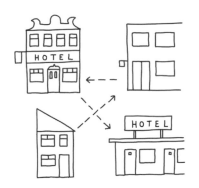

STAYING IN A
DIFFERENT HOTEL
EVERY NIGHT

DEALING WITH CRITICISM
FROM ARMCHAIR EXPERTS
ON SOCIAL MEDIA

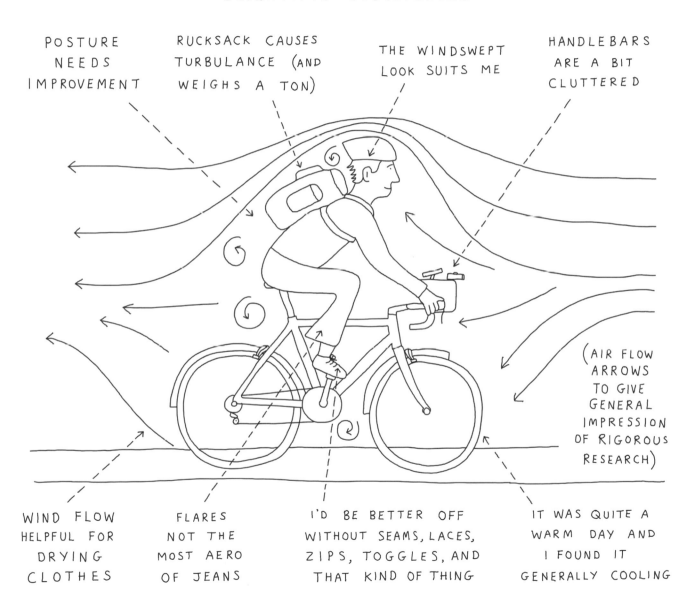

THE WIND TUNNEL

SCIENTIFIC DISCOVERIES

POSTURE NEEDS IMPROVEMENT

RUCKSACK CAUSES TURBULANCE (AND WEIGHS A TON)

THE WINDSWEPT LOOK SUITS ME

HANDLEBARS ARE A BIT CLUTTERED

(AIR FLOW ARROWS TO GIVE GENERAL IMPRESSION OF RIGOROUS RESEARCH)

WIND FLOW HELPFUL FOR DRYING CLOTHES

FLARES NOT THE MOST AERO OF JEANS

I'D BE BETTER OFF WITHOUT SEAMS, LACES, ZIPS, TOGGLES, AND THAT KIND OF THING

IT WAS QUITE A WARM DAY AND I FOUND IT GENERALLY COOLING

TODAY'S ROUTE PROFILE

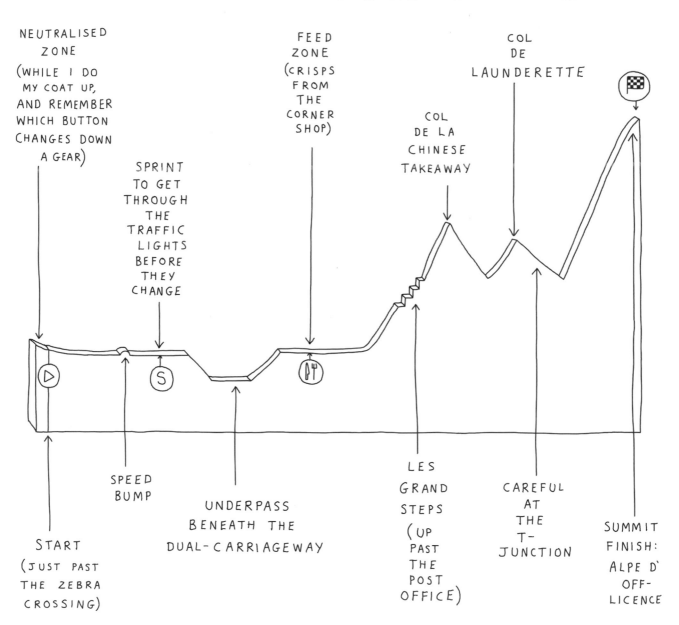

NEUTRALISED ZONE

(WHILE I DO MY COAT UP, AND REMEMBER WHICH BUTTON CHANGES DOWN A GEAR)

SPRINT TO GET THROUGH THE TRAFFIC LIGHTS BEFORE THEY CHANGE

FEED ZONE (CRISPS FROM THE CORNER SHOP)

COL DE LA CHINESE TAKEAWAY

COL DE LAUNDERETTE

SPEED BUMP

START (JUST PAST THE ZEBRA CROSSING)

UNDERPASS BENEATH THE DUAL-CARRIAGEWAY

LES GRAND STEPS (UP PAST THE POST OFFICE)

CAREFUL AT THE T-JUNCTION

SUMMIT FINISH: ALPE D' OFF-LICENCE

CYCLING SAFETY

WE ARE ASKING THE PRIME MINISTER TO IMPLEMENT THE RECOMMENDATIONS OF THE 'GET BRITAIN CYCLING' REPORT. WE WOULD LIKE:

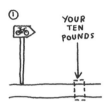

① £10 PER PERSON PER YEAR SPENT ON CYCLING

② SUFFICIENT FUNDS, GIVEN THE PROPORTION OF JOURNEYS BY BIKE

③ CYCLING TO BE FUNDED FROM VARIOUS BUDGETS

④ CYCLING PROVISION IN ALL NEW DEVELOPMENTS

⑤ IMPROVED GUIDANCE TO HELP PLANNERS INCLUDE BICYCLES

⑥ CYCLE ROUTES ALONG AND ACROSS MAIN ROADS

⑦ CYCLE-FRIENDLY IMPROVEMENTS ON LOCAL STREETS

⑧ NEW REGULATIONS FOR THINGS LIKE BICYCLE TRAFFIC LIGHTS

⑨ 20 MPH SPEED LIMITS IN TOWNS, AND 40MPH ON MANY LANES

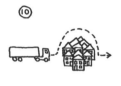

⑩ HGVS LIMITED AT PEAK CYCLING TIMES. AND MADE SAFER

⑪ TRAFFIC LAWS ENFORCED AND OFFENDERS BROUGHT TO JUSTICE

⑫ CYCLE TRAINING AT ALL SCHOOLS

⑬ AFFORDABLE CYCLE TRAINING FOR ADULTS, SO THAT MORE TRY IT

⑭ CYCLING TO BE PROMOTED AS SAFE AND NORMAL

⑮ A PLAN TO BE MADE (PLEASE KEEP US UPDATED)

⑯ A NATIONAL CYCLING CHAMPION (ADVISOR)

⑰ TARGETS. HOW ABOUT 10% OF ALL JOURNEYS BY 2025?

⑱ PEOPLE IN GOVERNMENT APPOINTED TO TAKE THE LEAD

DANGER

RIDING MY BIKE IS TOO DANGEROUS, SO NOW I JUST SIT ON THE SOFA

<u>THE DANGERS OF SITTING ON THE SOFA</u>

SPILLED TEA

ATTACKS BY ANIMALS

OVERCONSUMPTION OF SNACKS

FALLING PICTURES

STRAINING BACK LOOKING FOR LOST ITEMS UNDER THE CUSHIONS

SITTING ON THE SOFA IS TOO DANGEROUS, SO NOW I JUST RIDE MY BIKE

INJURIES CAUSED BY THE NEED TO OCCASIONALLY VACUUM

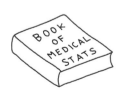

ILLNESSES CAUSED BY INACTIVITY

THE CYCLE ROUTE

ALL OBSTRUCTIONS* ARE REMOVED FROM THE PATH OF THE CYCLIST

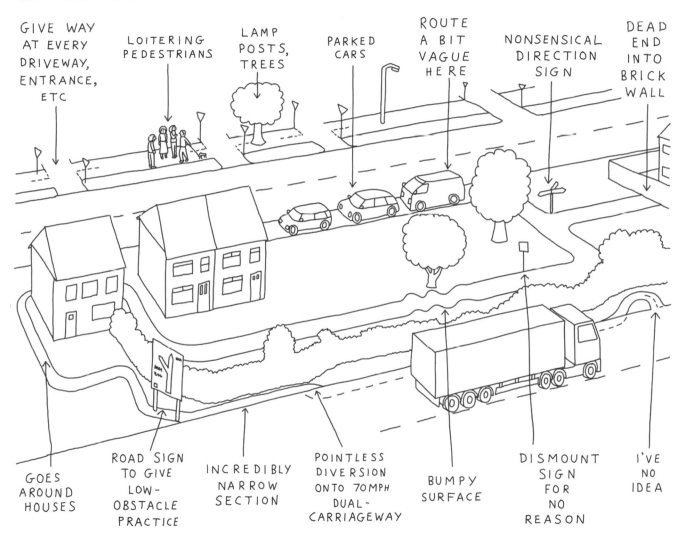

GIVE WAY AT EVERY DRIVEWAY, ENTRANCE, ETC

LOITERING PEDESTRIANS

LAMP POSTS, TREES

PARKED CARS

ROUTE A BIT VAGUE HERE

NONSENSICAL DIRECTION SIGN

DEAD END INTO BRICK WALL

GOES AROUND HOUSES

ROAD SIGN TO GIVE LOW-OBSTACLE PRACTICE

INCREDIBLY NARROW SECTION

POINTLESS DIVERSION ONTO 70MPH DUAL-CARRIAGEWAY

BUMPY SURFACE

DISMOUNT SIGN FOR NO REASON

I'VE NO IDEA

*EXCEPT TRAFFIC, PEDESTRIANS, PARKED CARS, SIGNS, TREES, IDIOTS, ETC, ETC

PLEAS

TO MY FELLOW CYCLISTS

GENERAL
IMPRESSION
OF
UNLIT
CYCLIST

IF IT'S DARK USE LIGHTS
(YOU CAN BORROW MINE IF YOU WANT)

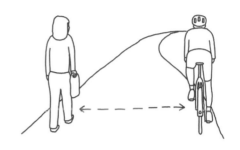

GIVE PEDESTRIANS PLENTY OF
SPACE ON SHARED PATHS
(AS YOU EXPECT CAR DRIVERS
TO DO FOR YOU)

STOP FOR RED LIGHTS

DON'T DROP GEL WRAPPERS
(INCLUDING THE TORN-OFF END BITS).
THIS ISN'T THE TOUR DE FRANCE

THE HIRE BIKE

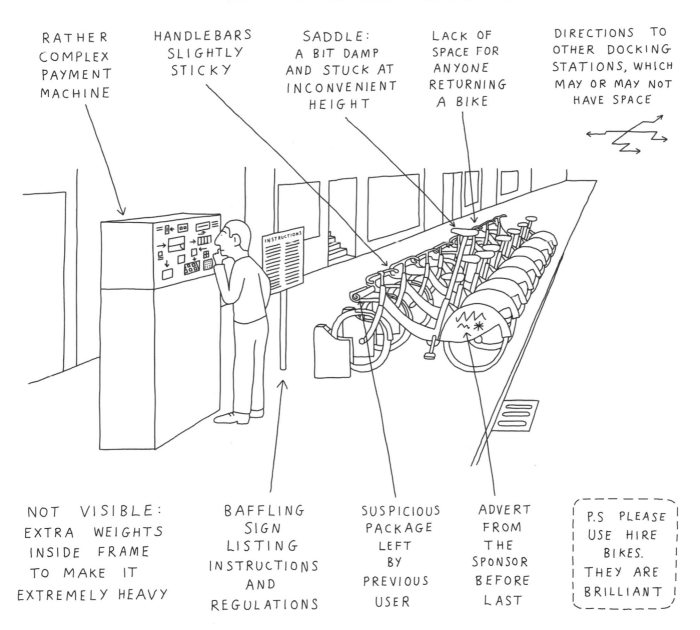

RATHER COMPLEX PAYMENT MACHINE

HANDLEBARS SLIGHTLY STICKY

SADDLE: A BIT DAMP AND STUCK AT INCONVENIENT HEIGHT

LACK OF SPACE FOR ANYONE RETURNING A BIKE

DIRECTIONS TO OTHER DOCKING STATIONS, WHICH MAY OR MAY NOT HAVE SPACE

INSTRUCTIONS

NOT VISIBLE: EXTRA WEIGHTS INSIDE FRAME TO MAKE IT EXTREMELY HEAVY

BAFFLING SIGN LISTING INSTRUCTIONS AND REGULATIONS

SUSPICIOUS PACKAGE LEFT BY PREVIOUS USER

ADVERT FROM THE SPONSOR BEFORE LAST

P.S PLEASE USE HIRE BIKES. THEY ARE BRILLIANT

THE FIXIE

THE WIDTH OF THE HANDLEBARS IS VERY IMPORTANT

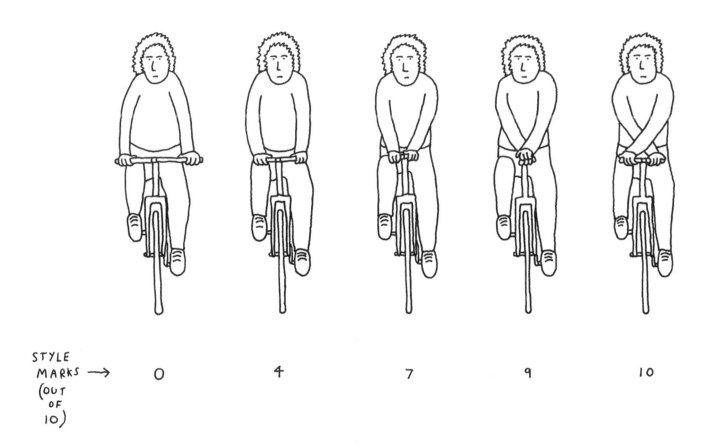

STYLE
MARKS →
(OUT
OF
10)

0   4   7   9   10

HAZARDS

CHOOSE YOUR ROUTE

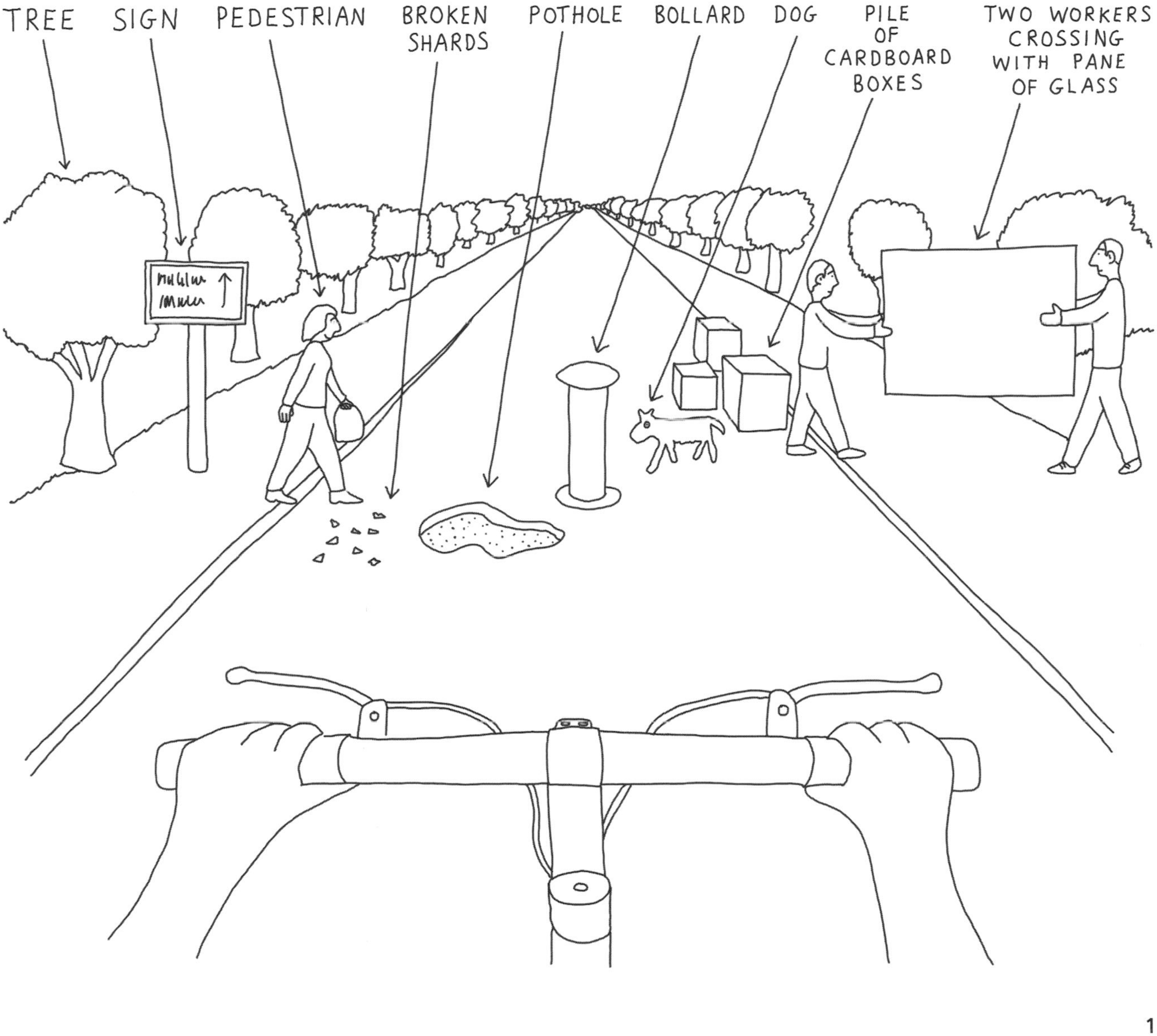
TREE
SIGN
PEDESTRIAN
BROKEN SHARDS
POTHOLE
BOLLARD
DOG
PILE OF CARDBOARD BOXES
TWO WORKERS CROSSING WITH PANE OF GLASS

WHY PEOPLE DON'T CYCLE

HILLS?

MOST CAN BE TACKLED BY CHANGING DOWN A GEAR OR TWO

THE WEATHER?

THEY MAKE REALLY GOOD WET WEATHER KIT THESE DAYS

TOO SLOW?

OTHER FORMS OF TRANSPORT: BACK THERE SOMEWHERE

IT CAN BE MUCH QUICKER FOR SHORT DISTANCES AND IN TOWNS

THE MAIN REASON: IDIOTS WHO MIGHT KILL YOU

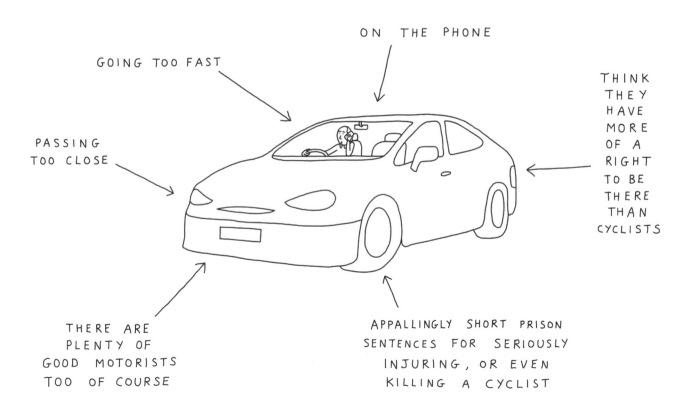

ON THE PHONE

GOING TOO FAST

PASSING TOO CLOSE

THINK THEY HAVE MORE OF A RIGHT TO BE THERE THAN CYCLISTS

THERE ARE PLENTY OF GOOD MOTORISTS TOO OF COURSE

APPALLINGLY SHORT PRISON SENTENCES FOR SERIOUSLY INJURING, OR EVEN KILLING A CYCLIST

LOCKING YOUR BIKE

BUY A DECENT LOCK

BIKE RACK

RAILINGS

PEOPLE ARGUING ABOUT HELMETS

LOCK THE BIKE TO AN IMMOVABLE OBJECT

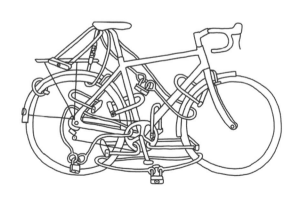

LOCK EVERY PART TO EVERY OTHER PART

IT DOESN'T HURT TO LOCK YOUR BIKE NEAR TO A FAR MORE EXPENSIVE-LOOKING ONE

CARRYING THINGS

IT IS TRICKY

SPOILS THE
LOVELY
SLEEK LINES
OF
YOUR
BIKE

RACKS AND PANNIERS

SWEATY
BACK

RUCKSACK

NOT GOOD FOR
BULKY PROVISIONS

OVERSIZED
BATON

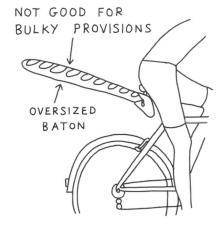

SADDLE BAG

RISK OF
SAGGING

JERSEY POCKET

NOT GOOD FOR NARROW
GAPS OR IMPULSIVELY
SPRINTING FOR
VILLAGE
NAME
SIGNS

TRAILER

RECOMMENDED
WHERE
POSSIBLE

DOMESTIQUE

CHILDREN

HOW TO TAKE THEM WITH YOU ON A BIKE

CHILD SEAT

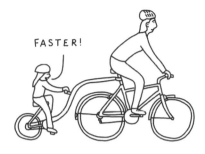

FASTER!

TAG ALONG

TRAILER

CAR LEFT!

CARGO BIKE OR TRIKE

LET THEM DO THE WORK

THEIR OWN BIKE

KEEP THEM ON A LEAD

TRANSPORTING A BIKE

USING YOUR CAR

PROS AND CONS OF VARIOUS METHODS

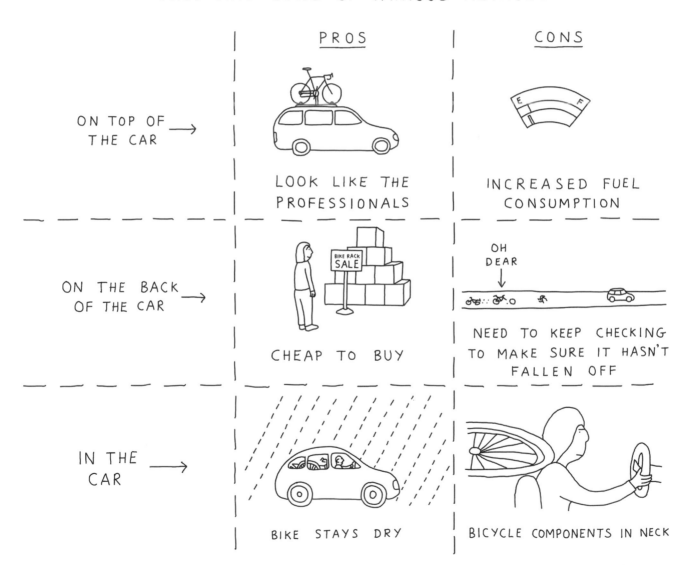

	PROS	CONS
ON TOP OF THE CAR →	LOOK LIKE THE PROFESSIONALS	INCREASED FUEL CONSUMPTION
ON THE BACK OF THE CAR →	CHEAP TO BUY	NEED TO KEEP CHECKING TO MAKE SURE IT HASN'T FALLEN OFF
IN THE CAR →	BIKE STAYS DRY	BICYCLE COMPONENTS IN NECK

MINOR MISDEMEANOURS

THAT MOST OF US HAVE PROBABLY COMMITTED AT SOME POINT

DING
DING

UNINTENTIONALLY SCARING
A PEDESTRIAN

SLIGHT
WOBBLE

CARRYING SHOPPING IN
AN INADVISABLE MANNER

IT WAS
REDUCED

WEARING CYCLING KIT THAT
WE LATER REGRETTED

PERFECTLY ACCEPTABLE

SLOWING DOWN THE TRAFFIC
FOR A SECOND OR TWO

(IN THAT YOU HAVE EVERY RIGHT TO
BE THERE, PAY FOR THE ROADS LIKE
EVERYONE ELSE, AND ARE HELPING TO
REDUCE CONGESTION AND POLLUTION)

CYCLING TO WORK

FEWER SICK DAYS

EXERCISE

MORE ALERT

BETTER SLEEP

NOT AS MANY FUMES AS IN YOUR CAR

IT'S REALLY GOOD FOR YOU

FUEL BILLS

GYM MEMBERSHIP

WELCOME TO THE GYM

IT SAVES MONEY

MILE FOR MILE IT IS AS SAFE AS WALKING

IN FACT GARDENING IS MORE DANGEROUS

IT'S SAFE

TRAIN

CAR

MILES & MILES

WALKING

POGO STICK

IT'S BETTER THAN OTHER FORMS OF TRANSPORT

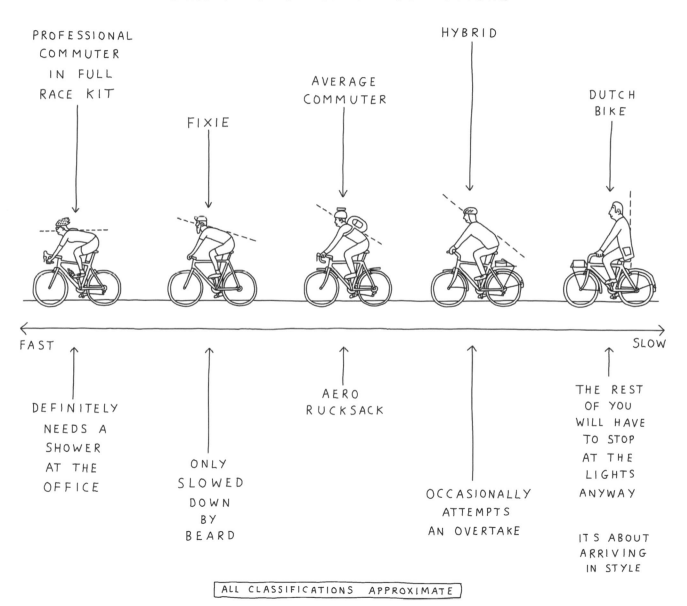

COMMUTERS

CLASSIFIED BY SPEED AND POSTURE

PROFESSIONAL
COMMUTER
IN FULL
RACE KIT

HYBRID

AVERAGE
COMMUTER

FIXIE

DUTCH
BIKE

FAST

SLOW

DEFINITELY
NEEDS A
SHOWER
AT THE
OFFICE

AERO
RUCKSACK

THE REST
OF YOU
WILL HAVE
TO STOP
AT THE
LIGHTS
ANYWAY

ONLY
SLOWED
DOWN
BY
BEARD

OCCASIONALLY
ATTEMPTS
AN OVERTAKE

ITS ABOUT
ARRIVING
IN STYLE

ALL CLASSIFICATIONS APPROXIMATE

MARGINAL GAINS
IN THE OFFICE

USE AN
AERO MOUSE

TRY NOT TO BE THE ONE DOING
ALL THE WORK AT THE FRONT

KEEP A FLAT BACK

CHOOSE OPTIMAL SWIVEL-CHAIR
WHEELS FOR THE CONDITIONS

KITCHEN

STAY HYDRATED

THE CYCLING COMMUTER

WHO FORGOT TO BRING A CHANGE OF CLOTHES

THE FOLDING BIKE

1.

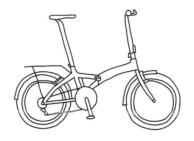

2.

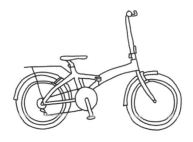

3.

4.

5.

6.

7.

8.

9.

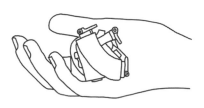

TIME TRIALLING

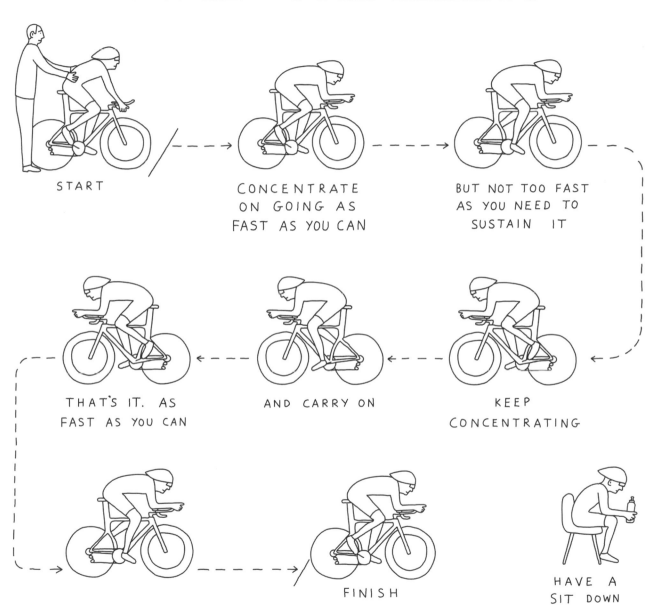

START

CONCENTRATE
ON GOING AS
FAST AS YOU CAN

BUT NOT TOO FAST
AS YOU NEED TO
SUSTAIN IT

THAT'S IT. AS
FAST AS YOU CAN

AND CARRY ON

KEEP
CONCENTRATING

FINISH

HAVE A
SIT DOWN

TRACK CYCLING

THE VARIOUS EVENTS

PURSUIT

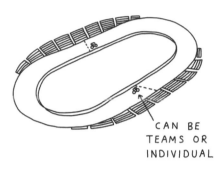

CAN BE
TEAMS OR
INDIVIDUAL

START ON EITHER
SIDE OF TRACK. SEE
WHO CAN CATCH WHO

KEIRIN

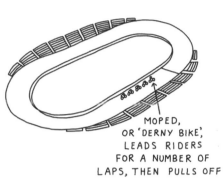

MOPED,
OR 'DERNY BIKE',
LEADS RIDERS
FOR A NUMBER OF
LAPS, THEN PULLS OFF

CHASE A MAN ON A
MOPED, THEN GO AS
FAST AS YOU CAN

SPRINT

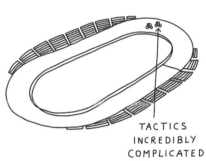

TACTICS
INCREDIBLY
COMPLICATED

GO SLOWLY. REALLY
REALLY SLOWLY. THEN
FAST. REALLY REALLY FAST

ELIMINATION RACE

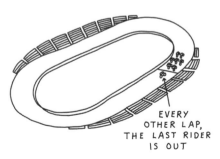

EVERY
OTHER LAP,
THE LAST RIDER
IS OUT

MUSICAL CHAIRS
FOR BIKES

POINTS RACE

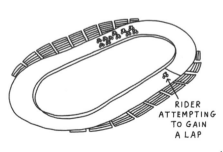

RIDER
ATTEMPTING
TO GAIN
A LAP

BIG BUNCH. TRY TO
GET A LAP AHEAD, OR
WIN OCCASIONAL SPRINTS

OMNIUM

SCRATCH
RACE
(FIRST OVER
LINE WINS)

PURSUIT

ELIMINATION
RACE

TIME
TRIAL
(TIMED CIRCUITS)

FLYING
LAP
(TIMED CIRCUITS
WITH A RUN UP)

POINTS
RACE

A BIT OF EVERYTHING.
WINNER IS THE
BEST OVERALL

MOUNTAIN BIKING

20 REASONS TO LOVE IT

IT'S
FUN

NO CARS
OR FUMES

UNEXPECTED
CHALLENGES

GREAT IN A GROUP
OR ALONE

FLYING DOWN A
TRAIL IN THE WOODS

(SCENE
WITH
TREES.
ARTIST'S
IMPRESSION
OF
SILENCE)

PEACE AND
QUIET

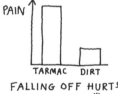

FALLING OFF HURTS
A BIT LESS*
*USUALLY

THE RIGHT KIT NOT
SO IMPORTANT

FRIENDLY
PEOPLE

IT TAKES YOUR
MIND OFF LIFE

ADRENALINE/
EXHILARATION

CHUNKY
TYRES

STUNNING
SCENERY

JUMPS

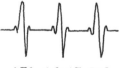

ITS GREAT FOR
FITNESS

BEING CLOSE
TO NATURE

SUSPENSION
(OR NOT - YOUR CHOICE)

THE CHALLENGE OF
IMPROVING TECHNIQUE

EXPLORING
NEW PLACES

RELAXING AFTER
A RIDE

CYCLE TOURING

ALL YOU
NEED
IS YOU

AND
YOUR
BIKE

(AND SOME PANNIERS   A TENT   TENT POLES

A SLEEPING BAG   A MUG   A BOWL   CUTLERY

FOOD   A STOVE   A TIN OPENER   A WATER BOTTLE

A PAN   A PHONE   A CHARGER   A TOOTHBRUSH

TOILETRIES   A TOWEL   MONEY AND CREDIT CARD

UNDERWEAR   CASUAL CLOTHES   EXTRA LAYERS   SHOES

GLOVES   SOME TOOLS   A PUMP   A LOCK   A TORCH

A FIRST AID KIT   AND AN ADDITIONAL SUPPLY OF TASTY SNACKS)

RIDING MY BIKE

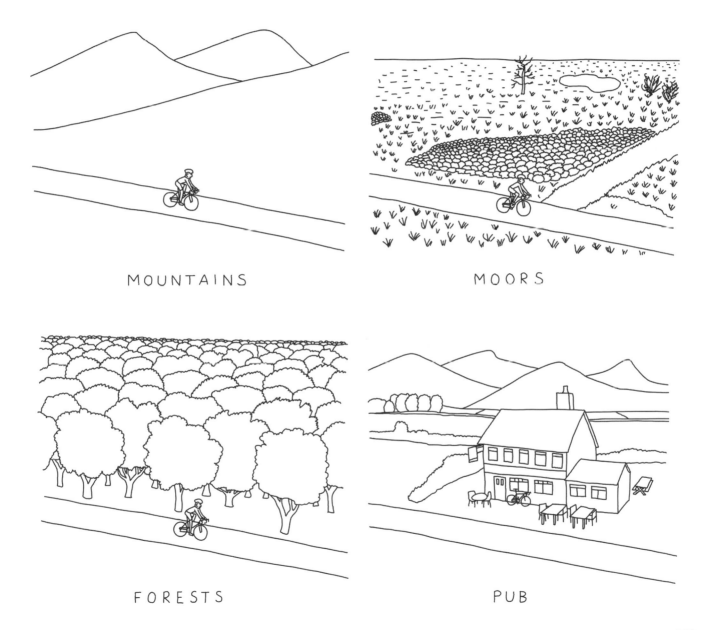

MOUNTAINS

MOORS

FORESTS

PUB

PREPARING FOR SUMMER

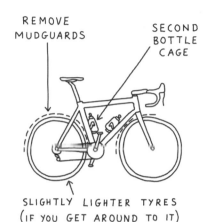

REMOVE MUDGUARDS

SECOND BOTTLE CAGE

SLIGHTLY LIGHTER TYRES (IF YOU GET AROUND TO IT)

MAKE MODIFICATIONS

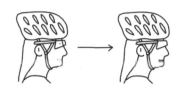

REPLACE YOUR CLEAR GLASSES LENSES

THE 'WHY DON'T THEY FIT?' STRAINING EXPRESSION

SEE WHETHER YOUR SHORTS STILL FIT

HIBERNATING DO NOT DISTURB

DUST OFF YOUR BEST BIKE

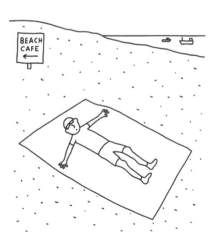

BEACH CAFE

TRY TO GET A CYCLIST'S TAN

CONTEMPLATE TAKING OFF A LAYER OR TWO

PREPARING FOR WINTER

LOOK FOR YOUR GLOVES

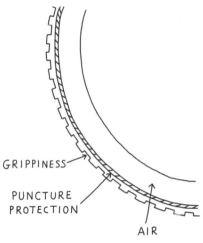

GRIPPINESS

PUNCTURE
PROTECTION

AIR

CHANGE YOUR TYRES

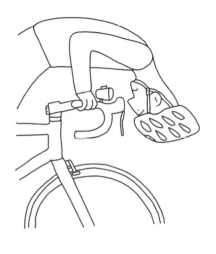

SEE WHETHER YOUR
LIGHTS STILL WORK

GLOOPY
OIL

APPLY THICKER
CHAIN LUBE

EXTRA
TOOLS,
TUBES,
ETC

SOUP

MAKE SURE YOU ARE
CARRYING ALL ESSENTIALS

LAG YOUR PIPES

THE 12 (CYCLING) DAYS OF CHRISTMAS

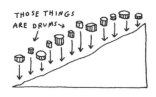

12 DRUMMERS DRUMMING
(ON ALPE D'HUEZ)

11 PROS PUNCTURING

10 CYCLOCROSS RIDERS
A-LEAPING

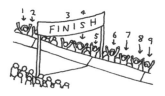

9 LADIES DANCING
(AT THE FINISH LINE)

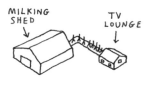

8 MAIDS-A-MILKING
(BUT TAKING A BREAK TO
WATCH THE BIKE RACING)

7 SOIGNEURS
A-SWIMMING

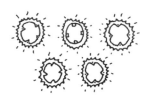

5 GOLD CHAINRINGS

4 COOLING BEERS

3 FRENCH MEN
(OUT ON THEIR BIKES)

2 WINTER GLOVES

AND A BIDON
IN A PEAR TREE

6 RIDERS A-LAYING
IN THE ROAD

SANTA'S BIKES

CARGO BIKE: FOR ALL
OF THE PRESENTS

MOUNTAIN BIKE: FOR
REACHING THE GROTTO
IN THE WOODS

FOLDING BIKE: TO
TAKE ON THE TRAIN

HAND CYCLE:
BEATS RUDOLPH—
DOESN'T NEED CARROTS

PRESENT
IN
JERSEY
POCKET

ROAD BIKE: FOR
SPEEDY DELIVERIES

KID'S BIKE: SURPLUS
LEFT OVER FROM
LAST CHRISTMAS

FIXIE: MAINLY USED BY
SANTA'S TRENDY
BROTHER IN LONDON

PRESENTS

FOR THE CYCLIST WHO HAS EVERYTHING

CHAMOIS
CREAM

EMBROCATION
(DOES THIS STILL EXIST?)

DECAF
SHAMPOO

CYCLING-SPECIFIC
TOILETRIES SET

CLIPLESS SLIPPERS

HANDLEBAR RIBBONS

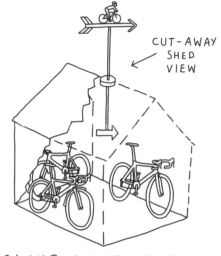

CUT-AWAY
SHED
VIEW

CYCLING WEATHER VANE
(POINTS AT RIGHT BIKE FOR
THE CONDITIONS)

THE
CYCLING
CARTOONIST

BOOK WITH
CARTOONS IN IT

A LARGER REAR SPROCKET
(FOR THOSE STRUGGLING
WITH THE INCLINE)

MATCHING
HIS-AND-HERS KIT

£20

A GIFT
TOKEN

BAR TAPE

A TOKEN
GIFT

RIDING A BICYCLE

HOW IT CAN CHANGE THE WORLD (SLIGHTLY)

NO OIL
TO RUN IT

NO
FOSSIL
FUEL
EMMISSIONS

NO
FUMES

IT'S SUSTAINABLE

IT REDUCES CONGESTION

BRILLIANT
IDEA

IT GIVES YOU SPACE TO THINK

SO EASY TO
STOP FOR
A CHAT

IT'S GOOD FOR COMMUNITY

INDEX OF CONTROVERSIES

IN THIS BOOK

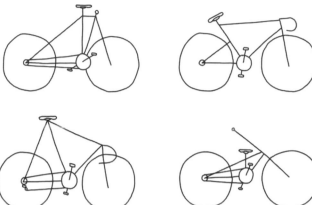

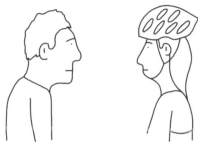

UNFEASIBLE FRAME GEOMETRIES

TOO MANY HELMETS /
TOO FEW HELMETS

BIKES WITH BRAKE
LEVERS, BUT NO
VISIBLE MEANS
OF STOPPING

HELMET
MIRACULOUSLY
STAYING IN
PLACE WITHOUT
STRAPS

CHAINWHEEL ON
WRONG SIDE

ODD
NUMBERS
OF
DIGITS

TOO
MUCH
LYCRA

MAN
WEARING
BIG COAT
IN PROTEST

IT DOESN'T MATTER

WHETHER
YOU
HAVE
THE
RIGHT
BIKE

LIGHT

THIS YEAR'S
MODEL

SHINY

BIT
OLD

A FEW
CREAKS
AND GROANS

STILL
GOES

WHETHER
YOU
HAVE
THE
RIGHT
KIT

AERO
(BUT
WITH
CONVENIENT
POCKETS)

JEANS
AND
T-SHIRT

WHETHER
YOU
LIVE
IN
THE
RIGHT
PLACE

SPECTACULAR

EVERYDAY

WHETHER
YOU
HAVE
THE
RIGHT
LEVEL
OF
FITNESS

JUST RIDE

ACKNOWLEDGEMENTS

Thanks to everyone who has bought this book! I hope you've enjoyed the cartoons and that you've found something for you, no matter what your level of cycling involvement is.

I'm grateful to all who support my cartooning activities: those who commission me to draw cartoons, those who buy licences to use my work, and those who email, tweet, share, comment, repost, and generally help. A particular mention to Paul Handley and the *Church Times* for whom I've drawn a weekly cartoon for 12 years, and without whom my cartooning career wouldn't have got past the start ramp.

Thanks to Bloomsbury for making this book possible, and to Charlotte and Sarah for their enthusiasm for the project, patience as I nearly met my deadlines, and the way they have guided me through the process.

I'm very grateful to anyone who has commissioned cycling cartoons, some of which appear in this book. In particular to Tristan and Stuart at Mpora, who were the first to put in a repeat order for cycling cartoons. Also Cycling Weekly, road.cc, Cycling UK, Evans Cycles, Cyclefox, Elephant Bike, Traidcraft, and others.

I rely heavily on friends to help me in the creation of cartoons. Many people contributed specific ideas that I used as I wrote and drew these diagrams during 2016. In no particular order (and I will have forgotten some – apologies): Mark Newitt, Sam Donoghue, Alastair Jones, Sam Wakeling, Steve Tomkins, Bex Lewis, Kate Wareham, Tim Hall, Alison Crutchley, Nigel Brown, Alex Gowing-Cumber, Tim Mayo, Sara Batts, Hannah Dobson, Malcolm Mackinnon, Steven Buckley, Sarah Strong. Also the members of my highly secret Cycling Cartoon Ideas group on Facebook.

I'd like to thank my family for their love and support. And particular mentions to friends for encouragement during the drawing process: Tom Wateracre, Naomi James, Andrew Graystone, and the community at the Fishermen's Chapel, Leigh-on-Sea.

Most of all I'd like to thank Charlotte, my wife, who has helped me with so many aspects of this book, has to cope with my weekly inability to have any ideas, and without whom this quite simply wouldn't have happened.